T0090602

Heartfelt

A Journey Through Transplantation

JOSEPH PANZA

iUniverse, Inc.
New York   Bloomington

Heartfelt
A Journey Through Transplantation

iUniverse books may be ordered through booksellers or by contacting:
iUniverse

1663 Liberty Drive
Bloomington, IN 47403
www.iuniverse.com
1-800-Authors (1-800-288-4677)

ISBN: 978-1-4401-7389-9 (pbk)
ISBN: 978-1-4401-7390-5 (ebook)

Printed in the United States of America

iUniverse rev. date: 9/11/09

Contents

Acknowledgements

The writing of *Heartfelt* was an outgrowth of a website, or blog, developed at a time when my world was crashing in around me. I was losing my beloved wife and had no idea what lay ahead. I never intended to write this book. It started out just as a way to keep people apprised of Jean's health while she was going through an ordeal that could cost her her life. Because this is now a book, things obviously changed. Our story has a happy ending. So, as we embrace our good fortune, we do so knowing that many have helped, in large ways and small, but all in the spirit of loving us.

We are grateful to so many people. We fear that leaving anyone out will hurt feelings. Certainly that is not our intent. Those we mention were there for us at a time when so much was at stake and when some days were a blur of emotion, expectation and doubt. If we forgot to mention you by name, please forgive us for that. We were a bit dazed.

First, we wish to thank our children: our son, Chris, who was at Yale-New Haven Hospital at my side the day of the transplant and who endured living with a father who was beside himself with fear and anguish at the thought of losing the woman who had made a life with him; he was a rock; Stacie and Amy, our daughters, who happily are trained in nursing and pharmacy and who besides being beautiful and smart, were able to come from Colorado on the red-eye more than once in the days after Jean's surgery and who were by our side at the hospital and at home as we learned to traverse a new landscape of constant medical demands immediately following transplantation, creating medication protocols and setting up systems to keep everything running smoothly; and Joe, our oldest son, who visited and was so supportive of us both in his light-hearted and blessed way, easing tensions with his spirit, sensitivity, joviality and humor.

Next, to Glenn Miele, our friend, who works cheaply setting up websites (amazing what a chilled Bombay Sapphire can get him to do) and who is always willing to get computer things to work as they are supposed to. I "blame" him for the simple little website, howsjean. pbwiki.com, being transformed into a book, something I never expected or intended it to become. His wife, Aimee, visited Jean in the hospital on many occasions, as did so many others. Betsy Lewis represented the Hideaway, our local hangout. Adrienne Livingston cut Jean's hair while she was in the hospital and brought DVDs for us to watch when the days and nights got long. Maria and Frank Purdue, my sister and brother-in-law, Barbara and John Elward, Jean's sister and brother-in-law. Friends and co-workers of Jean's at the First Congregational Church of Old Lyme and others: our friends and colleagues were a wonderful diversion on those days when time was interminable.

Needless to say, to all the doctors and nurses of Yale-New Haven Hospital who treated Jean both before she received her heart and after, Drs. Jude Clancy, Joe Brennan, Don Botta, Woody Lee, and Stuart Katz, we send our thanks. To Joan, Noreen, Cheryl and Dorene, you were wonderful and prompt in answering all our calls and questions. Your patience was and is appreciated. We don't know all the names of those who attended the OR when Jean was transplanted or who flew the plane and helicopter to get the heart to the OR in time to be certain all would go just like in the textbook, but we thank you, whoever you are. To the nurses who cared for Jean before her transplant, particularly Mary and Kendra, and all the others too many to name, we send our thanks and sincere appreciation. A special note of thanks to the Intensive Care nurses who, after transplant, cared for Jean so wonderfully and so lovingly with such professionalism that was reassuring and comforting, especially those first few days post-transplant. I owe my sanity to your reassurance when I called frantic at obscene times of the evening that first night and morning to be sure Jean was all right. To Frenchie, Jean's soul mate in waiting, who encouraged Jean to go for walks, while she too was herself confined waiting for a new heart all those long weeks and who was successfully transplanted soon afterwards. Thanks for keeping Jean in step with the "program."

But, this book would not be complete without the wonderful strangers who allowed Jean's life to go on. In the throes of what can only be described as the worst possible time of their lives -- losing a child, they decided to donate his tissue and organs so that his life would continue to mean something and live on in the lives of others. His memory is now eternalized in our family as well as in his. Paula Flint, the mother of Drew Doucet, a 21 year-old young man whose death made Jean's renewed life possible, is one of us now. Paula's decision to let Drew go on living in others is heroic, wonderful, inspiring and beyond what mere words can describe. To her other children, Jared and Hayley, who made Drew's wishes known during what for them had to be a terrible time, assured their mother: "Drew would want this."

To each of you, we express our deepest gratitude and *heartfelt* thanks. Your love for Drew lives on in Jean and we cherish his and your gift to her and me. God has blessed us and we pray that God's blessings will always be upon you. You are forever in our hearts and Drew is a part of our family, as are you.

There are a few other people we met after Jean's transplant who have been helpful in ways directly related to the publication of this book. Tom and Joanne Kasprzak, authors of their own love story captured in their book, *Plain Vanilla with Rainbow Sprinkles,* a story about their daughter Mary, born with Down Syndrome, who at age sixteen became a donor and saved five lives in their unselfish act of love. They inspired and encouraged us to get our story out. Teri Brunski, who volunteered to design the cover for *Heartfelt,* was one of the first to read the manuscript so that she could get its flavor for the design message. Her encouragement meant a lot too. Her skill as an artist is apparent when you look at the cover of this book. It is said, you cannot judge a book by its cover, but I believe you can judge some things by a book's cover—the skill and talent of the artist, the audience and the theme. We think Teri got it right. And from an author's perspective, I need to say thank you to the staff at iUniverse: Amy He, who stayed with me from the first inquiry till the very point of deciding to publish, when Jessica George and Cherry Noel took care of my endless questions. Thank you so much for squiring me through this experience. To Kathi Wittkamper, in editing, thank you for your thoroughness and able assistance through the final stages to get this book out to the public. You were able and willing.

Finally, I wish to thank Andy Watkins, my son-in-law for his photographic expertise so that I had the correct dots per inch configuration needed for photographs used in the book.

We urge all who read *Heartfelt* to spread the word about organ donation. Miracles can happen, but we must remind ourselves, and each other, that we are interconnected and interdependent on one another in ways we may have never thought about. Encourage everyone to donate. In that spirit, we wish to tell you that any proceeds from the sale of this book will be donated to Donate Life Connecticut and New England Organ Bank, a chapter of United Network for Organ Sharing (UNOS) to help in their educational efforts to bring greater awareness of and fuller participation in organ donation.

Paraphrasing Gandhi, we all can be the miracles we seek.

Introduction

At bottom, *Heartfelt* is a love story although not in the conventional way that love stories are told. There are strains of that, as you will see. But, it is a love story that transcends the Hollywood genre. *Heartfelt* demonstrates how love, expressed and then extended by strangers can lead to the salvation of another family. One family faced with its own tragedy becomes another family's deliverance. A donor family's love for a family member -- a son, a brother, a loved one -- makes it possible for another human being, unknown and distant, to live on. Ultimately, those two families meet. Bonds form that could never have been formed without the experience of death. You will see how one family's greater humanity, through the perseverance of siblings and their determination to make their brother's legacy a lasting one, coupled with a mother's dedication to her beloved son and family love come to the rescue of total strangers.

This is a true story of life and death and what is possible when we choose to love unconditionally and how such love reaches across a terrible void and touches even those we have never met but whose lives we hold in our hands.

How we are truly interdependent on one another. How, whether we realize it or not, we are all connected in some way only to find that out as our lives play out.

Jean and I had married young in June of 1968; I was 22 and a graduate student finishing my master's degree in counseling; she was just 20. We had dated for three years and were madly in love during the 60s when the Viet Nam war was raging, riots were a regular occurrence in our cities; the political scene was pretty unstable, people were fighting for their civil rights and the right to vote. The year we were married we saw Dr. King murdered, Bobby Kennedy assassinated and watched our nation being torn apart by disagreement over the war and other serious issues. In light of all that turmoil, we decided there were no good reasons to wait to get married if the world was falling apart anyway. We were young, naïve perhaps, filled with love and passion. We just went where our hearts took us. It was perhaps not the right time, but it was right in every other way. Now, over 40 years later, we are still best friends, lovers and even more delighted that we have stuck it out for better or worse, in sickness and in health. And that is where this story takes you—through sickness and health but not in the usual way.

We were the best of friends and our love for each other was profound even from the first. When you're young, you never anticipate that you will grow old and face the challenges that age and health may present. Oh sure, you say those words, "for better for worse, for richer or poorer, in sickness or in health till death do us part" but you don't dwell on them—until you have to.

We became parents of our first child, our son Joe, one week before our first anniversary. Our second child, Stacie, was born fifteen months later, then Chris, two years after that; and, finally Amy was born two years later to wrap up our family.

During the children's early years, Jean had begun to have mild symptoms of tachycardia, mitral valve prolapse, arrhythmia and assorted heart related ailments. Doctors always assured us these were "normal" post partum ailments that afflicted many women. We believed them at first but we silently knew that they could be wrong. Jean became more seriously ill in the 1990s, after we moved to Connecticut. Her heart failure began at an uncertain time. We cannot pin down exactly when or how it began or what may have caused her decline. Doctors call this idiopathic disease. That's a fancy term for "darned if we know." She was diagnosed with congestive heart failure and the very first time we heard the term *transplant* occurred when we received a business card and a letter from the Yale-New Haven Hospital Transplant team. That got our attention, but still we never thought it would come to that. It did. On All Saints' Day, November 1st, 2007.

But I am getting ahead of myself just a bit. Around Jean's birthday in August 2007, following a routine ultra sound, we learned Jean would need a heart transplant! After spending years with declining heart function and health, her heart was in its last stages, producing not enough pumping efficiency to keep her body from filling with fluids that threatened to drown her. After receiving, over the years, first a pacemaker, then a pacemaker/ stimulator, and then eventually a pacemaker/stimulator/ defibrillator, nothing seemed to be helping. She was out of mechanical or technological options. Nothing short of a heart transplant could save her life. It is there that this journey begins. Within a month of that office visit, Jean was on her way to Yale-New Haven Hospital to begin the work up for transplantation, but before she was very far along, she was rushed to the ER at Yale, admitted and this journey began.

It is through *Heartfelt* I hope to provide an inside look at what our family experienced not as a way to prove heroism, for that is not the case on our end, but so that anyone who has not been down this road may be able to read our journey and learn from it as a way to prepare yourself if someone you love faces the likelihood of a transplant.

When, in September of 2007 Jean was hospitalized and put on the transplant list, we knew we were in a battle that we had to face realistically and with the knowledge that time was running out. When Jean entered the hospital, her many friends and our families, our children and others were concerned about her desperate and declining condition, about her emotional state and her psychological well being. At the beginning of what was a growing prospect of long days ahead while we waited, it became apparent that we needed to find some way to keep everyone apprised as at any moment things could speed up and there would be little time to get out the word. After visiting Jean at the hospital, I would arrive home to so many voice-mails, all asking, "How's Jean?" that I quickly realized there was not enough time to answer everyone. I came to the realization that this was going to be an experience I had to handle creatively or risk offending those who love Jean. I felt an obligation to communicate and I had to do it in such a way that everyone could be a part of this life-altering experience. We had no idea where it would take us. Or how it would end. We were strangers in a new land. We had children and grandchildren who lived far away, friends in other states and different time zones across the country. There had to be a way to simultaneously keep them all in the loop.

With the help of a friend, we created an website, largely unedited, and I pledged to everyone through announcements at the First Congregational Church of Old Lyme, Connecticut, where Jean worked, to spread the word that I would keep them informed via the website. I pledged to give them as well as family and friends any news and I would faithfully update the website each day as Jean and I progressed toward what we hoped would be a positive outcome. Of course, at the time, we had no firm or reliable reason to be assured that a positive outcome would indeed happen. We knew that far too many people died waiting for a donor to be found. Sadly, this fact continues to cost lives as donation is still far behind the need that is so apparent. Even though we were reassured, time and time again, by the doctors and nurses that everything would be fine, we had days when things seemed dark and gloomy. Nonetheless, we also held on to the hope that with so many people caring, praying and wishing, we might just be able to realize that hope. We had faith, but like most humans, our faith was shaky at times and at other times completely left us. Others could help us get it back when we needed to get it back. And, we needed it … a lot of the time.

Over the course of what became weeks and then months, the website became a refuge and my journal as well as a way to keep people apprised of how Jean was doing. Maintaining the website saved me from despair, it gave me renewed hope whenever I needed it and it became my ode to the woman I loved and wanted desperately to be saved from death from heart disease. We moved from fear of the present to a new fear of the future, ranging from being filled with anxiety, joy, pain, tears, despair, hope, darkness and light in varying degrees. Sometimes all in the same day!

Heartfelt did not start out as a book idea at all; it was originally a much simpler idea-- just trying to keep people informed as the days passed using the technology that we have today. Very soon after beginning, I recognized that I needed a place to seek refuge from my own fears, doubts and pain in seeing this drama unfold before my eyes, watching and waiting as the woman I have loved since I was a young man got sicker by the day. Some days our hopes were raised, others dashed. I needed to keep her and everyone who knew and loved her, connected. That connectedness sustained us. The website was that place. I recommend this idea to anyone reading this book. Your website does not have to become a book, that is not for everyone and it was certainly not what I was thinking when this all began. But, it is a way to get and keep people connected and to feel the love and support of those who care for us. It can be used to heal! I never thought that would happen, but as I got caught up in doing it, I soon realized that it was my lifeline, my rock, my "quiet" place where I could put my emotions and feelings down, create some space to heal my heart and my soul, begin to believe that we'd be all right and that the road, while winding and torturous at times and turns, would lead us back home safely and on solid ground to move on in life.

Months after the website began, when Jean finally decided to shut down the website, that brought howls and even more pressure to produce a book, based on the website, written to help others who might have to face what we faced. The idea of a book came at the urging of the people who read daily updates on our hastily designed website and ultimately from some of the professional staff of the cardiac transplant team and other survivors we met at support group meetings after Jean's transplant. So many people encouraged me to publish this. I concluded that if there were indeed a need for such a book, I would give it a shot and see if I could turn our website into a useful tool for others. If it worked for us, why not see if it might assist others?

What follows, this book, derives directly from the website in hopes that it might be helpful to others going through the rigors of transplantation. It is chronological in that it begins at the starting point where Jean learns that she needs a new heart. (Imagine, if you can, how those words spoken out loud sound when they hit your ears?), but then wraps up post-website when so many other events made the fabric a whole cloth. So much that came afterwards was never fully anticipated; it was really quite unknown to us, but it makes this book more readable and gives it the lifting power that the website alone would not have been able to give. The connectedness of the human condition plays out more and more as you will see.

Maybe *Heartfelt* can answer questions, ease worry, arouse curiosity about this medical marvel and more broadly educate others. Maybe it can build closeness, heal the spirit and offer hope in a time when that may be all you can hang onto.

The later chapters turn this into what even the website could never have done because the website was mine and mine alone, as time wound its way toward culmination. In these later chapters two families are brought together. It was there that we came to see how those on the other side of our joy whose family faced the other questions, the other fears and doubts, came to our rescue. In death, the person they loved made our lives so blessed. In the process of meeting each other for the first time we could finally put to rest so many unanswered questions that helped us to understand how salving the pain of one, lifts and inspires the other and teaches us all once again that there is no greater love than giving of one's life to save another. And, there is an ironic twist of fate that will become apparent when you get there. How my career and the donor's life intersect is an amazing example of those things we can only look to the heavens to better comprehend. Indeed, how we are all somehow connected. You will read Jean's words as she describes events from her perspective, which is clearly quite different from mine. She was at the center of the vortex; I was peripheral to it although there, holding her hand, literally and figuratively. Our children wrote of their collective experience to shed light on how family members experience this ordeal of a mother fighting to stay alive. We had hoped to have Paula Flint (Drew's mother) tell of her perspective from the other side of the equation, when a parent faces what has to be the most difficult, heart-wrenching decision of all, letting your child go, knowing that in his loss you might be helping another human being whom you might never meet or know. Paula at first was willing but later decided that she simply could not do so. We deeply respect her wishes, as we have come to know how painful and powerful her loss has been as she continues to find healing too. Nonetheless, happily for Jean and me and our family, we have met several times and shared ourselves and bared our emotions with one another. We have come to regard Paula, Drew, Jared, Hayley and Ron, Paula's large family, Drew's grandparents and the Amesbury cast of thousands as newfound and dear friends and family. We are now connected to them and there, as well.

Each transplantation experience is of course unique and personal. Our is ours and ours alone, but in the hopes that others may at least get a sense of what it is like, we share our experience so that we can in some small way give back. We have been where others may not yet have gone and we know that the power of information; love; concern; prayers and well wishing always makes for a better outcome, no matter the medical issue. We believe we are all spiritual beings having a human experience and that we humans are all interconnected to one another. We pray that if your family is going through this as you read this book, that your results are as wonderful and happy as ours have been. You are not alone.

It is in that spirit that we offer this, our *heartfelt* thanks to Drew, Paula, Hayley and Jared, and to all those who loved us, cared for us, prayed for us and visited us to lend support and encouragement. We know we have been blessed. And, to any of you reading this about to go through your own experience, know that we pray for you. Far too many people, children and adults, die each day waiting for organs and tissue that never comes because too many of us do not think of donating. Sad, but true. We can all save a life, even more than one, simply by donating.

As you read the website entries, you will learn through our eyes how transplant decisions are made, how the randomness of numbers plays such a part in how organs become available and just how tightly the coordination must be for all the stars to align. That it works is amazing even to this day.

Chapter 1 - Brief History
In Real Time, The Website & The
Journey Begin

Jean was first diagnosed around 2002 with Congestive Heart Failure (CHF) due to cardiomyopathy, a fairly common diagnosis that means the heart muscle is deteriorating and weakening thereby hampering the heart's ability to pump blood and assist in removal of fluids through the body's other systems, such as the kidneys, lungs etc. Since then, her heart had been deteriorating slowly but steadily until this summer (2007) when, on vacation at the Cape, she experienced pedal edema that seemed to set things in motion and augur badly for her. Since then, late June and early July, she began to experience increasing edema in her legs and other areas of her body until it became obvious she was unable to reduce fluid retention using medications and adjustments to her defibrillator/pacemaker/stimulator, which was implanted a while back. Weight gain indicated that she was carrying a large volume of fluid and her heart was unable to excrete it even with the device and medications she was taking. We received the first warning about a transplant at a check up following an echocardiogram later that summer.

Jean's Journal & Chronology of Events

(Readers are invited to visit the website: howsjean.pbwiki.com, to get a full visual effect of what was happening as it was being written. What follows here is a slightly edited version of the original for purposes of the book.)

Weeks 1 & 2 Like a Blur

On Monday, September 24, 2007, Jean was taken by ambulance from her office to the ER at Yale-New Haven Hospital (YNHH) at which time the decision concerning a heart transplant was moved along rapidly. We were made aware of this likelihood shortly before but had just begun that very morning the start of the work up to the transplant process, which is usually done on an outpatient basis. Jean's heart failed to cooperate so we were directed to the hospital immediately. There, we were told that Jean would not be able to leave the hospital without a new heart and the process of transplant eligibility began in earnest on an inpatient basis. Then .... Following all the various and many procedures Jean was told that indeed she was a candidate for transplantation and would be designated as 1A, the highest urgency category. We were gladdened by the news that due to Jean's size and blood type, B, she was likely to get a heart sooner as B is more rare and therefore has less competition for recipients. She can also accept the heart of anyone from teenager to adult between 105 and 250 pounds. Of course, a 'too large' heart would be unable to fit her body so we hope for a smaller heart. Meantime, she was able to shed 15 lbs of excess fluids in just a few days with IV meds and other medications more potent and in larger dosages than what she could use outside the hospital. She is monitored in every possible way, wired and telemetrically watched by computers all around the CCU.

10/6/07 DAY 1 on the list. Jean was officially placed on the transplant list today. HEART AVAILABLE. Later the same day, we were advised that a heart from New Hampshire was available, and it was being cross-matched with another person in Boston. It almost never happens that a person is listed and on the very same day a heart becomes available so we were ill prepared for what followed so soon after the news of Jean's status being decided. Later in the day, we learned that the other person in Boston was the recipient. We were not disappointed because we never had the chance to fully comprehend the whole process and so we never got our hopes too high. But now we realize how this might work. A phone call is made and the process begins to unfold like a dramatic TV show, only it is a real drama and sadly another family must face the unenviable reality of losing their loved one at the same time deciding to save Jean's life, and the lives of others, by donating organs. We are well aware of the significance of this terrible dilemma and pray that whoever makes that awful decision does so with the knowledge that we are grateful for their God-like wisdom and grace.

This weekend, dear old friends, the Sloans and Dalys came from NJ to visit; Barbara, Jean's sister, and her husband John came too, even staying overnight to spend a weekday visit with Jean, certainly not to enjoy scenic downtown New Haven! Maria Purdue, my sister, and her husband Frank, came by a couple of times during the week and on the weekend. Other friends from Jean's church office, former co-workers, and Hideaway patrons, and umpire friend of mine stopped by to see her. So, we are blessed by these people

3

being sure that they express their caring and support for her, which makes the days go by a bit better if not faster. Flowers have been received, but we urge you to hold off on sending flowers. We would rather see you send a donation to the organ donor organization in the USA to help promote organ donations everywhere. Candy, however, is all right, as Jean continues to enjoy her Jelly Bellies, a package from Amy & Karen in CO, Swedish Fish and Dots from Chris, our son, and Alia, his girlfriend. Jean has a DVD player so I bring her movies she can watch when the TV stations get stale.

Week 3

10/10/07 DAY 4 All signs remain positive, Jean is at 5 - 1 in the Yale ICU which has no phone service at the bedside but she can be reached on her cell phone. Remember, we are on EDT, for those of you calling from out of state. Her care has been stellar and of course she is wooing everyone with her "big heart" and loving graciousness. She is already sharing recipe books with the staff and enjoying the camaraderie that develops in a place like this. She even wangled a refrigerator out of the hospital so she can keep things cool! You know Jean; she has to feel at home. She even joked that she wanted me to bring some furniture from home. At least I think she was joking!

At any moment, we hope to get the call that says a heart has been found, Jean is the best match for that heart and that it is en route to New Haven. And, a few hours later, Jean will have new life with a new heart. Keep the candles lit!

10/11/07 DAY 5 Jean's kidney function has shown marked improvement, which is good news since this will be vital to the success of the transplant. The stay at Yale has improved many things and the well-monitored environment has allowed Jean's body to recover generally although her heart continues to be the central focus, of course. She reported today that her weight is down to 128! She could probably get into her wedding dress again. Friend Aimee brought Jean a new boa so when I mount her picture on the website she will look "mayvelous dahlin!"

Daughter Stacie Watkins arrives today for a visit with Jean and me. She comes from CO, for a few days to make sure her mom and dad are doing okay. Chris meets her at the airport in Providence RI. It will be good to have some company from CO, our old home territory. Niece Jamie Mercer and husband Galen came from VT to see Jean today. Gale from the University gifted me spinach bread from Venice Bakery, but I think that goes home with me! Too much salt for her; but not for me.

Jean posed for her first picture today, the boa was Aimee Miele's contribution and the hat came from the back seat of the VW Beetle Convertible. We had a very small budget for this shoot!

10/12/07 DAY 6 No news on the heart transplant today, but Jean continues to hang in there. Her patience is remarkable in the face of the intrusiveness of all the different readings and tests and blood samples that she has to give each day. It seems like there are miles of tubes and wires connected to her yet she smiles through the morass and keeps the staff laughing. Visits today from Joni and Emily form FCCOL lifted her spirits and Stacie and I were there for a large portion of the day. Later, when she tired, she needed to rest and we left her in bed and resting as comfortably as possible. It wears on her that this is dragging out, but it has really been a short time, except not really for her. It seems interminable. She has to endure the discomfort and pain of being alone and away from home. We keep praying that the heart we need will soon be here.

10/13/07 DAY 7 Another good day. Total weight loss is now 20 lbs. Stacie and I, along with Chris, visited most of the day and Jean was in very high spirits, sassing me and ripping anything that came to her quick wit. Barb and John came up again from NJ for a one-day visit, which we appreciate so much. Kendra was Jean's nurse today and took great care of her, even letting her shower when she wants. The little things mean so much. Jean walked and exercised a bit so that she can prevent atrophy while she waits. We brought Halloween decorations for her room and lots of candy corn and other staples of the season. Dinner at Anthony's with Stacie was ordered by Jean and John the bartender sends his regards along with so many others. The pizza, as usual, was spectacular. Tomorrow, we start again.

10/14/07 DAY 8 Rev. Cathy Zall came by to see Jean today as did former neighbors and still friends, the Livingstons, Tracey, Jamie, and Adrienne, who was kind enough to cut Jean's hair so she could be more comfortable and need less primping time each day. Jean has been able to ambulate around the ICU as many as three times, rare in this unit, and now has some leg weights and hand weights we brought her to keep her strength up. She got a pedicure and some snazzy polish too. Of course, being Jean, when I arrived today, the candy dish we put together for her was out at the nurse's station, picked clean except for a few loose ends. On our way out, we got a "thank for my hips" comment from one of the staff. That's Jean, always sharing and making sure everyone has something to eat. No new medical news as she continues to remain in good condition considering her heart issues. No fever, good vital signs, lots of IV fluids and DoButamine drips. Her nurse, Kendra, has kept up the fine care that Mary, her primary nurse, has seen to give Jean. We are so grateful for their great passion and commitment, not just for Jean, but also for everyone on that unit. Splendid people, all. Daughter Stacie, herself a nurse, is equally impressed with

Jean's care as am I. Sadly, tomorrow is Stacie's last day for this visit although she will return when Jean has her new heart and is going home with it. Daughter Amy, the family pharmacist, will also be helping out dear old dad when the time comes for Jean to come home. Everyone has agreed to pitch in. Son Chris, who had planned to escape the cold weather this winter and go to Phoenix, has decided to stay in CT for the time being so he is also available to help out whenever we need his strength and love for us. Stacie and Amy pitched in and bought Jean a digital photo frame with about 100 pictures that flash non-stop on screen to keep her connected to everyone. She has family pictures from our last vacation at the Cape as well as some historical pictures. Great comfort. Thanks for the memories. Andy loaded the disk with the photos from his collection.

Week 4

10/15/07 DAY 9 Jean had a very good day today. All her "numbers" look really solid and so we just have to wait some more. That's the way this works. Stacie departs in the morning so the farewell was a bit emotional tonight, yet her visit was a great, refreshing change of pace. She leaves just in time as she discovered the stores in New Haven and a Starbucks! Next time she visits, their sales are sure to increase. She was a big boost to me, too, as we got to share many father-daughter moments while traveling back and forth to Yale. She and Jean got to do a lot of girl stuff like nails and hair. Her boys, Luke and Holden, made the sacrifice of sending their mommy to CT and poor Holden cried long distance every day missing his mommy. Andy, her husband and our wonderful son-in-law, deserves so much credit for going it alone for 5 days being house dad and holding down the fort while she was here.

10/16 DAY 10 No news to report. A quiet day of rest.

10/17/07 - HEART AVAILABLE - DAY 11 Jean was informed that a heart might be available. The heart was in Boston. This occurred at 6 AM. We were initially told that final decision would be made around 11 AM. At 11:20 AM we still had no definitive word. That came and went with no closure and the deadline was extended to 5 PM. Jean called me on my cell phone to say that the deadline had been extended to 5 PM, so we are on standby right now. It is now 2:36 PM so we don't have too much longer to wait. Noreen, the coordinator on duty today, came in to see us and told us that the heart in question is still inside the operating room awaiting the removal of the other organs, especially the liver, which is being dissected for two transplants as we write this. When that is done, the other organs will then be harvested with the heart being last to be removed. It is an O blood type heart, which is compatible for Jean even though she is B. Jean is next on the list if for any reason the first in line recipient is ruled out, Jean is a go! Not great odds, but we're in the game. It is now 9:30 and still the wait goes on. Why? We don't know. Jean has been on hold since 6 AM and still we have no definitive answer about the heart. This tension is unbearable. But we are the beholden to the way this works. Today, Jean's nephew Matt visited, and a friend from FCCOL, Marge. Yesterday, Revs. David Good and Carleen Gerber visited. Jean just called at 9:37 PM and she is eating for the first time since yesterday. The heart is going elsewhere. Another false alarm. It has been the longest day so far. We will fight another day!

10/18/07 DAY 12 We have now been through two dry runs at this. Each has taught us that this is hardly a standard operating procedure (nothing about this is 'standard') at all. So many variables enter into the decision-making that at any moment things can be changed, matches can be found and people can be juggled on the list at the primary center (in both cases for us, Boston). And, we have learned that what we believed and were told about hearts being taken last from a donor is not true. Hearts are taken first, which makes yesterday's events even harder to decipher, as the process was interminably long. But Jean endured it well and finally got to eat late last night after going all day (from 6 AM to past 9 PM) without food and having not eaten since the day before. Her weight, already down 22 pounds, is certainly making her hungrier as her appetite has improved now that she is no longer laboring to breathe. She was issued an apology by the transplant physician but he had no real part in the delay since it was all being done in Boston and he was, like we were, waiting to hear by phone what the status of the heart was. So, we continue. This may have been the toughest day so far, but God bless Jean, she held up better than I did. We learned today too that we have been laboring under a misconception about how hearts are harvested. They are not the last organs removed as we thought. Hearts are taken earlier. This confuses what happened yesterday even more since at 6 AM Jean was alerted to the possibility the heart would be forthcoming so that she would not eat in the event she was to receive the heart; yet, when time began to slip by, the situation became more muddled as we were under the impression that the heart would be last to be removed. Apparently, what we were digesting in the way of information was not accurate or we misunderstood it. Nonetheless, the delay was excruciating. We are learning to take this a step at a time as we experience these hurry up and wait trial runs.

10/19/07 DAY 13 Nothing new to report on Jean's condition as it remains the same. Alia, Chris and I went to visit today. Alia brought Jean an electronic solitaire game to use. Once we figured out how it worked, it was fun to use. Jean can stay in game shape for the casinos this way. Alia showed Jean the technique to play and completed a very difficult triangle puzzle. Julio Crespo, our nephew through marriage, came by to surprise Jean and he brought a beautiful floral arrangement from his children Julia, Mercy and Duke, the dog, to lift Jean's spirits. His visit was very special to Jean. She also received a beautiful robe as a gift from one of our many "other children" from CO, Allison, one of Stacie's dearest and oldest friends, who sent a warm and toasty robe from LL Bean. Jean wore it and announced it warmed her, both inside and out. Jean walked the ICU three times around and she lifted some weights too to keep her arms and shoulders in shape. The PT staff left some exercises for Jean to do so we worked on those a bit. It is just a matter of time before we know the outcome of all this waiting. Another day is finished.

10/20/07 DAY 14 Another pound lost but all indicators are good, as Jean's numbers remain strong. Visits from John and Barbara on their return from RI with old friends, Tom and Jean Martin, who regaled us with their worst cruise ever story. Jean spoke of getting her new heart this weekend so I am hoping she has had a premonition, but we have nothing official. Jean has made friends with another person named Frenchie who also is waiting for a transplant, so they walk together sometimes and visit daily. Frenchie likes crossword puzzles so Jean has shared her crossword books with Frenchie and Jean has taken up knitting, which she hasn't done for a long time. Filling the time is the hardest thing. So, we wait while another day fades to dark. The new photo above is of a gift bear whose apparel was based on the photo of Jean, the Martins and Elwards presented it today. Don't they make a nice pair, Jean and the lookalike bear? When you squeeze her hand she sings, "girls just want to have fun." The bear, not Jean!

10/21/07 DAY 15 Chris and I visited Jean for a few hours today. She and I played rummy but we were not able to finish the game as a surprise visit from Adrienne Livingston around 6 o'clock interrupted play. We will get back to this heated match. Jean was holding her own and competing hard. Then, in a surprise move, she asked me to bring Scrabble to the hospital so she can try her hand at that. I welcome the challenge. We played Scrabble a lot when we were newlyweds and despite taking her lumps then, she wants to go again. I love her spunk! In another sort of karmic coincidence, while having dinner tonight with Chris, at the Hideaway, a man sitting next to me told me about his brother receiving a lung transplant last May; he now is playing golf and feeling terrific after what had to be an equally grueling ordeal. So, with these types of hopeful stories we are encouraged that this will all end well for us, too. While we were there, the McCrackens arrived and we had a short visit with them before we left the restaurant to head home to watch the Red Sox and Indians, one of who will take on our Rockies (our adopted favorite baseball team from our days in Denver)! Week 5 begins tomorrow with the hope still high as we await the possibility of a new heart for Jean.

WEEK 5

10/22/07 DAY 16 The gin rummy tournament continued today. Jean made a strong comeback to tie the series at one game apiece (she put up a better fight than those darn Indians did). But, Scrabble (a gift from Alia) begins soon and we will see how she fares in that milieu! She is asking for trouble in my world of words. There were more phone calls today offering support from Joe's friends from baseball umpiring as word has spread among that group of some of the finest men I know. Calls, cards and offers on "anything you need" came in today. Next time you want to kill the ump, remember these are some of the nicest people you will ever meet and they will give you the shirt off their backs. I know these men; they mean it! (Whether or not they have washed *that shirt in a year or more is debatable, but they offer it lovingly!) I miss them but have hung 'em up so my career is over in that sphere of activity, yet they continue to care about Jean and me, very kind and solid men, all. Jean really misses home so we are trying to bring her any touches of home we can. Five weeks away have taken their emotional toll, but her resoluteness inspires me. I draw strength from her, as I am amazed at her pluck and determination. After I left this evening, Connie Hurtt of FCCOL surprised Jean with a late visit for which I am grateful. This week the Rox and Sox get after it in the World Series and we await news of whether our son-in-law Andy and grandson Luke can get tickets for under a million dollars. We'd give anything to be there to witness the first World Series ever in Denver. I attended the very first Rockies game and it will forever be one of my favorite memories -- historic and so exciting. And, we wait on.*

10/23/07 DAY 17 Tuesdays are by far the worst days for us both. Jean has a weekly procedure for replacing the Swan-Ganz, which measures her heart's capacity to pump blood. To prevent infection, it is replaced frequently. This is painful and done without general anesthesia so Jean experiences the pain and later discomfort attendant to it. Plus, my schedule on Tuesdays is the busiest so that I am unable to get to her much before late afternoon between my two late classes, one at 3:15 and the last one at 7:35, which runs till 10:05 PM. If I have any scheduled counseling and advisement of students that is usually during office hours in the middle of the day or late morning, so it is really a tight day but a long, lonely one for Jean. We welcome any visitors on Tuesdays, especially early afternoon and early evening so Jean isn't alone so long. And, so far today, there is nothing new on the progress toward a new heart. It will happen when it happens.

At 1:20 PM Jean called me to say the Swan-Ganz insertion was over and she was back in her room resting. That's a huge relief!

10/24/07 DAY 18 Jean's Ganz was a bit painful today yet she did not complain. She was visited again by Wendy Kerpo from FCCOL, whose husband is also at Yale. Jean's niece, Jaime, stopped by on her way to Boston with a beautiful basket of daisies and other seasonal flowers. Today, we began the 'spring training' for Scrabble. Jean and I were both a little rusty having not played this for a long time so we eased into it. We enjoyed some good-natured teasing and eventually worked together to beat the game without regard for the score. It was good to see her competing and having fun. We laughed and cajoled while we played. Alia sent some more candy reinforcements that should get Jean, and the staff, through the next few days until I can make another run!

10/25/07 DAY 19 Nothing new medically to report today. Dan Junior, a friend of mine from umpiring, who works at the Yale Nursing School, dropped by with another cache of candy. I worry that when this is over Jean will need dental work! Aimee Miele came by again as she is wont to do faithfully each week and she too brought an assortment of candy with lots of licorice. We both enjoy licorice but we have so much it seems like too much at times.

10/26/07 DAY 20 The medical staff increased Jean's DoButamine again today as an added measure to keep her heart strong and to sustain her 1A status on the list. This raises concern that her defibrillator may trigger again, which is very frightening and quite uncomfortable for her. It raises Jean's anxiety level appreciably. Visits from Maria (my sister) and Frank Purdue, bearing a gift of an angel, and Tom and Marla Richardson of FCCOL, bearing a 20 Questions game, were highlights. Jean continues to receive cards and get wells from so many people and we are enriched each day with loving expressions of support that touch us deeply. A gift of a Scrabble strategy book brought by Wendy Kerpo is appreciated. Today's visitors made the day go by a bit faster than usual. Carleen Gerber too came by and we so appreciate the attention and love expressed by all who read the website and comment how this keeps them in touch with Jean even though she is not physically present in Old Lyme. Jean was in some discomfort from the Ganz again today. Percoset made it a bit more palatable but she was not quite herself today as this medication is very hard on the stomach. I know Jean is a trooper but the pain meds can't dim her pain as we would like and yet she takes it all in stride when I know I would have weeks ago thrown in the towel. Many of the cards are so inspirational. One reminded us that as each day goes by, we are closer to the end of this waiting. It is this kind of sentiment that helps get us through. Bless you all for the part you play in this saga of hope, love, determination and faith that it will end soon one day. Joni May's phone call was a lift for Jean as I watched her engage Joni in work related conversation. She admitted that she really misses the church office and all the people about whom she cares; she sends her love and generosity of spirit your way. After Joni's call, Jean rebounded some. When I left her tonight she was in some pain and feeling a bit uneasy but I pray she will be okay in the morning when I see her again. We learned that some hearts have been available but that they were not good matches. This process goes on behind the scenes, so we are not notified unless there is a chance that the hearts available are a match for Jean. So ...

10/27/07 DAY 21 Jean had a bad day today. Her nausea continued for most of the day as she tried to gut it out, but I implored her to get some relief so she could eat something. By the time I left tonight, she was eating a little soup and crackers and even had some candy so I think she was feeling a little better. Her spirits have been sagging a bit as she misses home terribly, just as we here at home miss her equally; but we are all aware that her return home is out of the question with all the meds she needs and the monitoring required to assure that her health is maintained while she waits. Maybe tomorrow will be better. Phone calls lift her spirits, as do visits from others. I am there every day so my presence does not have the same lifting effect as the visits of others. I understand that so I prepare for her each day as though it will be the last day we have to wait. Each day that goes by we know is a day closer to the end game. It is just a random event that triggers this and then we're off and running to the finish line. Tomorrow we start again.

10/28/07 DAY 22 A better day today. Jean's nausea abated and she was feeling a little more spry, even walking the unit again and eating better. I brought some pizza from a local pizzeria and that seemed to sit well with Jean. She loves pizza! Of course, she can't have it too often, but a piece now and then is all right according to the nurses. We played co-op Scrabble some more and read together, she her book, I the papers and Time Magazine, *so we filled the time while "watching" football in the background. The day went by quickly and when I left, Jean was in pretty high spirits for the most part. More cards came in and she has received so many that I have collected them in a basket I keep at home so that Jean's room is not so cluttered. It is much easier to keep house when I can bring things home and keep them safe so when Jean comes home, all those wonderful gestures of support and expressions of love and healing can be seen again but in a very different light. Jean has received myriad cards ranging from humorous and profane, Mass cards from Catholic friends, scapulas and novenas from others, and get-wells from dozens of people, many from FCCOL, and from our friends in general. She has gotten electronic games* for poker, black jack, and 20 Questions, Boggle and Scrabble board games. Jean has received fresh and natural flowers as well as silk flowers along with stuffed animals, so her room has begun to take on its own personality. Books and magazines are also in plentiful supply.

Another week begins...

WEEK 6

10/29/07 DAY 23 Jean remains the first Type B recipient on the New England regional list, but several hearts have been unable to be acquired due to limitations of various hospitals' ability to cross-match her blood with donor blood types. We learned today that there was a heart in MD that might have been a good match for Jean, but the donor hospital had no way of matching Jean's blood even though Yale agreed to fly Jean's blood sample to MD to do the cross-match. Either time or inadequate services were a factor. Today, Jean had another med added to her regimen to improve her heart function just a bit, a small adjustment but one the doctors think she needs to secure her health in the meantime. This med will be added to the DoButamine she is now taking as a booster so that her heart keeps functioning as she waits. Today was a good day overall. Her spirits were good and her outlook remarkably bright as well. She continues to inspire me when I get down about how long she has been away from home and from me. The nights are especially hard for us both. Neither of us has slept very well since this began and so we have to endure this long separation with as much grace and strength as we can. Tomorrow the Swan-Ganz weekly insertion occurs again, so I expect her to have some pain and discomfort again. These weekly intrusive procedures cause some concern for infection and attendant discomfort so I worry about them each week. Last week, the doctors moved the Swan-Ganz to the left side of Jean's neck *to give her right side a break. This week they will stay on the left side. We'll see what the day brings.*

10/30/07 DAY 24 A very tough day today. Jean experienced great pain and was very dispirited expressing her pain and frustration in wanting to go home. Of course, she can't do that, but my heart ached for her suffering that she would voice such a sentiment. I tried to comfort her but she was despondent and not easily consolable. Tuesdays are like that every week. The Swan-Ganz was moved back to the other side of Jean's neck to the previous site in contradiction to what we were expecting. When I left her, and I hated doing so, I was concerned that she was so sad. It made for a long night.

10/31/07 DAY 25 What a rebound Jean made today. She was back to herself. She had visits from Joni May and Emily Fisher from FCCOL and she brightened and was back to her old self: joking, laughing, smiling and clowning around. I was uplifted to see her again being Jean as I know her to be. She had little or no pain and seemed to be well past the Tuesday trauma with a great recover. She has asked me to buy her a laptop so she can send e-mails and keep in touch with her legion of friends. I am shopping for this tomorrow and will soon have her hooked up and running at the electronic mouth. She is back! I think the missed Imperial Lancer reunion (Jean was in a drum and bugle corps in her youth) in NJ this past weekend we were planning to attend before all this began has triggered some interest from her childhood and teenaged friends from NJ and she wants to get in touch and respond to their get well wishes. So, we'll see if we can get hooked up. If we do, we'll send along her e-mail address.

11/01/07 DAY 26 It is 6:50 AM and Jean has called that there is a HEART. The surgeon and anesthesiologist are coming in to interview her for prep and we think this may be the day.

Oddly, today is Thursday and Jean had a premonition last week that her heart would come on a Thursday. Later that same day, one of the nurses said that it was her experience that many transplants occurred on Thursday. Jean and I locked eyes when she said that; we both sensed a Celestine Prophecy kind of moment had just occurred. I pray that this is that Thursday! We should know by noon if she is a "go" so Jean may well be in surgery at that time. So, if you're reading this this morning, get those prayers aimed high and skyward and call everyone you know to get us through this day. Our miracle may just be about to happen. Now I have to go get ready.

We have a heart!!!!!!

"This is the day the Lord has made, let us rejoice and be glad."

Jean went down to OR around 11 AM. At this time, 12:02 PM Jean is in the OR. We are waiting for the final word that she is all set to go. Needless to say, we are waiting anxiously. Chris and I have been here all morning. We moved her belongings out of the CICU room and now are on the CTICU on the third floor of the West Pavilion. We have already met one of the nurses who will be our contact during the day. We have been told that Jean is in OR. The heart, we think, is in transit from Boston. The consent forms have been signed and all signs seem to be positive. We were also alerted to the long shot possibility that even right to the very end, there is a slim chance that once Jean is under anesthesia, if there is anything wrong with the heart, she could wake up without it, but we resist the urge to think in those terms. Right now, our hearts are beating a little faster than usual as we wait to hear that the heart is in the surgeon's hands and that Jean is getting ready to be opened for the transplant. Pray with us.

I was amazed at the empathy and love all the nurses and staff, doctors and others showed Jean this morning. When the word spread, it was amazing how everyone came to see her and to wish her well. Alice, Jude Clancy, various nurses and all the regulars on the unit. I know that Jean has special quality of making people love her, but this really seemed extraordinary to me. The only day I didn't love her was the day before I met her, November 23rd, 1965. Since the 24th, I was hooked so I guess I have been the lucky one to have loved her before all these others got to meet her. Now they all know what I long ago knew -- she is amazing in her ability to touch people in a way they can easily attach themselves to her.

BULLETIN 1

Just received the call at 12:13, we are a go. The heart is coming from Boston, as the donor family has been very generous with many teams harvesting organs today, so Jean is all set to go. Now, we wait for the next call.

BULLETIN 2

Pat, the OR nurse called at 1:39 to say that Jean was being opened up and the heart looked good. The next time she will call is when the heart is beating in Jean's chest. So, here we go. Jean's last words when they put her under were, "I'm gonna shop till I drop!" Oy vey, now I have to get ready for that! Pat said that Jean is now in "la-la land," (that's not a medical term!) and really held up well before they knocked her out completely.

BULLETIN 3 "You Raise Me Up"

Dorene the social worker just came by at 2:15 to say the heart is in the air en route to Tweed Airport and should be here in a short time. This is so well coordinated they actually have the time of the surgery linked to the air travel. Jean is knocked out and ready for the procedure to start within minutes after the doctor walks into the adjoining OR with the donor heart. The actual operation takes about an hour for removal and insertion but the lead up and post-op can take up to 6 hours so we have a long day and night ahead of us. Typical of Jean, she has minimized any hassle for me. I had to cancel just one class today, but will not miss anything at work. She had all of our children on weekends too so you see how thoughtful she is! I guess that's her way of being sure I earn enough money for that shopping she likes to do! But, as long as I can, I will obey, I mean I will respect, her wishes.

I noticed that the day cleared as each hour passed and the sun shone brighter each time I looked out the window to ponder. This morning it was gloomy and cloudy, but right now it is bright and blue. I am as calm as I have ever been. It's odd I guess, but my faith is strong and my confidence in Jean's doctors and nurses has been based on observing how well she has been cared for during her weeks here. I know that right now they literally have her life in their hands, maybe even her heart itself, so I sense the magnitude of these moments with great calmness, yet I am carefree. Worrying now is fruitless, as it will do no good at all for Jean or me. One of my students, whose is quite aptly named Grace, just sent me this quote from Epictetus, "There is only one way to happiness, and that is to cease worrying about things which are beyond the power of our will." Imagine a student with that kind of insight! I guess that's where I find myself at this moment. I hope that Jean is as 'all right' as I am. I asked her to use as her last thought before she went under that I love her. I hope she did even as she was planning to shop!

Two of my favorite inspirational songs are Josh Groban's You Raise Me Up and You're Still You and right now as I wait, I am listening to his songs and I am moved to tears knowing

I am powerless to help Jean as I wait. Please go and listen to these two songs if you love someone and want to understand the way I feel about this remarkable woman I love. "After all, you're still you!" Nothing can change that, not a new heart, not a thing can make me feel differently. I was fine till now, but as the time winds on, I am feeling more anxious but still confident and hopeful. It is just the sentiments and the words of those songs that move me. They did even when Jean was not sick. Maybe I should listen to Little Richard instead. Nah, then I'll want to dance and drink, the other folks here in the waiting room probably wouldn't abide that behavior. Besides, there are no nearby Hideaways to run into.

11/3/07 By request here are some of the lyrics written by Josh Groban in You're Still You: *"Through the darkness, I can see your light … And I can feel your heart in mine … Your face I've memorized … In my eyes you do no wrong … I've loved you for so long … And after all is said and done … You're still you … I can feel your pain … Time changes everything … One truth always stays the same … And I believe in you although you never asked me to … I will remember you … And what life put you through … And in this cruel and lonely world … I found one love … After all … You're still you."*

The music for *You Raise Me Up* was written by Rolf Løvland, the lyrics by Brendan Graham. Josh Groban recorded the words that today helped me get through this darkness and brought me out the other end to the light: *"When I am down and, oh my soul, so weary … When troubles come and my heart burdened be … Then, I am still and wait here in the silence … Until you come and sit awhile with me … You raise me up, so I can stand on mountains … You raise me up, to walk on stormy seas … I am strong, when I am on your shoulders … You raise me up … to more than I can be."*

I hope this clears up any questions about why this music moved me so much the day of Jean's transplant. I could not have crafted songs more fitting than these on my best day much less that day.

BULLETIN 4

4:17 PM Jean's native heart is out and the new heart is going in. Noreen, one of the OR nurses, came out to report that Jean is doing beautifully and that within the next hour or so, the heart will be transplanted and hopefully beating on its own. We know now that it is the heart of a 21 year-old male. Gender is not a match issue so it does not affect the recipient. We're halfway through. Looking good.

BULLETIN 5 Eagle has landed! The new heart is beating.

At 4:45 PM OR nurse Pat just called, Jean's new heart is beating!!!!!

They are warming her up and I will shortly be going to see her in recovery. Thank you all for your prayers and well wishes. The day was made livable by your comforting expressions. Now the new normal begins in earnest and we will turn the page to see what comes next. People here in the waiting room have just applauded our wonderful news. People are amazing. Strangers relishing in your joy without knowing how much it means that we are not alone even in our darkest times. We are indeed interdependent in ways that take my breath away.

BULLETIN 6

6 PM Noreen came to see me about 6 PM to say that they were buttoning Jean up, tying up any bleeds and that the transplant was 'textbook'. I will likely not see her till 8 PM or so as they prepare to move her to recovery. Noreen prepared me for the visual I will see as Jean will be breathing on a ventilator and will have drains and tubes all over her. Those will be removed as soon as practicable. The next 24 hours are a critical time following such invasive surgery, but with all the indicators right now arcing in such a good direction, I am ever-confident that Jean will troop ahead on pace to be home as soon as she can. Those Christmas sales are right around the corner! I don't think I am going to complain about them this year! I will likely not be spending the night here as it is very unlikely that Jean will awake till tomorrow as it is late now and she is pretty heavily sedated. But, I want to see her just the same, so I will be here as long as it takes to see her at least for a few minutes.

BULLETIN 7

6:44 PM Dr. Donald Botta, Jean's surgeon, just came in to tell me, with a smile on his otherwise pretty serious face, that it "went perfect". He reported that the next 3 days will be critical and that the right ventricle will be the section of the heart that will be carefully watched, as it does not like to be without oxygen or be in a cooler! He has a sense of humor! And, our girl came through it with flying colors. I should be able to see her soon. I am just sitting here thinking how grateful I am and how great this next Thanksgiving is going to be. I feel certain that Jean'll be home in plenty of time to enjoy the holiday with us (and my birthday too) and be up and about and vibrant once again. Dr. Botta said the heart she got was a strong 21 year-old heart that will outlive me. I've just changed my mind about his sense of humor! It has been nearly 12 hours since Jean's call came in this morning and in that short span of time, we have witnessed modern medicine's startling technological mastery and the unbelievable resilience of the human body as well as the generosity of friends and even strangers -- all in a single day! Amazing, simply amazing! Life is a curious thing. And so precious. How can I top this day? I won't even try to imagine how I could. But, I know that I am forever marked by this as a time of tremendous reflection and appreciation for all that is humanly possible when minds and talents are put to use for the benefit of others. I am inspired by everyone I have come to know here but especially by Jean's courage and tenacity. She is my new hero and idol.

7:08 PM Daughter Stacie just told me that Holden, our grandson, came home from school today lyrically singing, "My Groma got a new heart." Six years old and writing music already, he obviously gets his "genius" from his grandfather's side of the family. (Hey Andy, how's that feel? Cardinal fan and Yankee hater!). Daughter Amy is on her way tonight from CO to be bedside when mom comes around in the morning.

8:30 PM I finally had a chance to see Jean and was so glad that I could. Donna, her nurse, let me see her for a brief few moments. She was resting peacefully, breathing deeply and resting well. She was just a few hours out of surgery but I could see that she was strong and resilient, her chest heaving strongly and powerfully. She was pretty beat up, with tubes everywhere, unconscious but beautiful in my eyes. I was not allowed to make any noise or to touch her, as I had hoped, so as not to startle her, but I know she knew I was there if even just for a few moments. I left and went to the Hideaway to meet Chris and Alia for a brief celebration and a bite to eat. When I arrived I was greeted with the news that Toni, our friendly bartender, announced to the patrons after my call, Jean's triumphal surgery and was told that the place erupted in celebration at the announcement. Jean would have loved that moment and will one day soon walk in and get the same celebration in person, of that I am sure. I could not have been more pleased to know that all those there felt so strongly about Jean as to applaud the news. I received some hugs and kisses from the folks there and was buoyed by their generosity of spirit and love for Jean. This woman is amazing, making friends wherever she goes. In what seems like an odd thing, I was congratulated by so many people, at the hospital in the waiting area, and afterwards in various phone calls and at the Hideaway, as if I had just had news of the birth of a baby, which is kind of like what happened in the sense that Jean has been reborn. I was discomfited that I, who had done nothing more than endure the day, should receive congratulations when I had really not done anything to earn them. Oh well, I guess people don't really know what else to say, so I accept their congratulations even though I had done nothing at all to earn them. Jean, the doctors, the nurses, the pilots, the ambulance drivers who transported her new heart, the donor's family and the others behind the scenes deserve my congratulations and eternal gratitude. It is they who deserve the kudos, not I. So, now at 11:15 PM, I am home and at ease. I can go to sleep knowing that Jean is resting safely, and with new and renewed life. What a magnificent day it has been! Thank the Lord, for His is the work of miracles every day and in every way. Now, I rest for the days to come. Thank you all for being there all day throughout this magnificent day of rebirth and miracle. To my children, my family, my friends, my colleagues, my students, the donor's brave and true family -- all of you -- I am forever indebted. God's grace is abundant and works in mysterious ways. He lifts me up, as do all of you. Thanks. Soon, I will have Jean back in my arms and I promise you and her that the first hug I give her will be from all of you with all my strength and love. You lift me up!

Chapter 2 - New Life, New Day - The Beginning

11/2/07 5:15 AM DAY 1 Jean made it through the night resting and recovering. I spoke with Donna, her nurse, late last night and then again this morning. She told me that Jean was a little awake and responding to questions already. I am going to be there when the visiting hours start at 7:30 so I can see for myself how she is doing. Daughter Amy is inbound on a redeye from Denver and due in around 5:30 AM. This website will now take a turn by concentrating on the post-operative phase of Jean's new life. I have gotten so much feedback about the value of this website that I feel compelled to keep it up until it is no longer of any value as it was before. That is, even after Jean is home and friends and family visit her, there may continue to be some value, different value, to speaking out about all that this presents. Someone even suggested that we publish this to help others who have to go through transplantation. I can't imagine that someone hasn't already done so, but who knows? I do know that writing this has been cathartic for me as a journal might be for someone doing that on an individual, but private, basis.

8:25 PM We have just returned from the hospital, daughter Amy and I, and we witnessed something absolutely extraordinary today. From early this morning Jean was on the ventilator, unable to speak; but by midday was off the ventilator, then on oxygen with a mask, and finally with just a cannula which improved her breathing. She had, by late today, begun to talk, drink water, eat Jell-O and Italian ice and give me orders about whom to call. I teased her and she teased me right back. When I joked about finally getting to eat for the first time since Wednesday and that she was going to eat Jell-O, she said, "There's always room for Jell-O!" She was doing Jell-O commercials! She was in quite a bit of pain but wanted to get off the morphine drip, as she didn't like the double vision it caused her.

Dr. Lee and Dr. Botta, the surgeon who transplanted Jean's heart, both were astounded by her progress. They are already planning her move to a step-down unit next week and planning to do the first biopsy a week from now with the likelihood that she might be home a week from Tuesday, November 13th! Can you imagine that? Amy and I got to listen to Jean's new heart via a stethoscope provided by her nurse, Melani, who was terrific in getting Jean though the first day. The heart was pounding strong and sounded like like a tsunami inside her chest. It is quite unbelievable that one day ago; Jean was fighting for her life and today she is speaking, joking, and breaking stones and back to her old self. When she was informed by me that her heart came from a 21 year-old male from Boston she shed tears and mouthed the words, "that poor mother." Just like Jean, she was pained for the loss of a mother she has never met and yet for whom she was fully empathic. She continues to amaze me.

Friends continued to call and write and for that we are so thankful. One friend, my buddy Arnie Mann, left a tearful message of joy and when I returned his call he again wept for joy at our good fortune. Even umpires with brass realize the impact of this. I will forever remember Arnie's emotional congratulations as if I had done something to earn his support! The truth of the matter is that we have only begun to endure this next phase. But, the beginning is in sight! Dr. Lee, who is as laid back as anyone, said to us, "it takes only 200 stitches to do a heart transplant!" He does these every day, so for him it is a day at the office. But for us, it is much much more than that. As we left, Jean said, "continue to pray," so we ask you all to honor her wishes. We can use all we can get. Now, we will get some sleep to face tomorrow.

11/3/07 DAY 2 6:25 AM DAY 2 Jean got through the first awake night with her new heart. Night nurse, Donna, said that Jean would not take any pain medication until the time the pain was so bad she finally gave in. She took IV Dilaudid but that did not help much, so with some more coaxing, she conceded, taking Tylenol and that seemed to take off the edge. Jean's stubborn resolve to be in control of her senses is another good sign. Pain meds make her feel so woozy that she dislikes the disorientation she gets from their use. I feel the same way about pain meds -- too weird a feeling. Pain seems more natural than a dazed sense of reality. Donna said that each time she went in to check Jean's IVs, Jean would awaken even when she did not make any noise. One time, Jean asked her, "how's **my** heart?" I am adding the emphasis on the word **my** for a reason. Jean is already treating the heart as hers! Yesterday, her reaction to the heart was at first great sadness for the donor and his mother, last night she asked about her heart. I think this is important in the sense that she has embraced her new heart as being a part of her. When we visit later today, I will be curious to see whether she is eating solid foods and sitting up. I imagine she will very shortly be looking for a contraband slice of pizza that'll have to wait till we get off the CTICU! The hospital does not baby heart transplant patients; they get them up and moving.

Jean has already gotten her chest pillow for coughing and has exercises for breathing she has to do every hour, so they are trying to build her back up quickly. No more lying around. Dr. Lee did say that Jean's quick progress was very likely assisted by the good shape she was in when the heart finally came in probably as a result of the hospital stay that she had in preparation for the heart. Her body was well-prepared and as healthy as could be thanks to the great care she got on 5 - 1 CICU with Mary, Kendra, Jocelyn, Lissa et al who showed such great concern and took such wonderful care of Jean. Getting off all that body fluid and keeping her body strong. We owe them so much.

11/3/07 11:20 AM Jean is looking great. Sitting up and trying to get her appetite back but slowly. She did not eat her breakfast today; eggs are not her favorite food. Dr. Botta, the surgeon who transplanted Jean's heart, came by and he confirmed that Jean is very likely going to be moving early next week in preparation for being discharged. She'll go to the 4th floor where the step down unit is and then be on the road to discharge from there.

She reported she had a restless night of sleep and I don't think that will change until she gets home to her own bed and surroundings where no night nurses are coming in to check her every 10 minutes. Of course they have to do that as Jean is still in the critical period. Today, Maila, the day shift nurse, will be removing the chest drains from Jean and she will be taking Jean for a walk! Chris, Amy and I spent some time with her. Her coloring is great, I thought she had on lipstick but she hadn't used any. She is still in quite a bit of pain but very soon, with the drains out, the oxygen cannula removed and the freedom to move about, she might begin to feel less discomfort except for that associated with the actual chest area. Rib pain is especially harsh. If you have ever cracked a rib, you know what I mean. She started on the immunosuppressant meds today and those did not sit well on her stomach, combined with not eating heartily, her stomach did not have much protection from the taste of that so she didn't tolerate it too well. All in all, she looks great, although not sleeping as well as we would like, yet is beginning to gain strength, her blood pressure and pulse are strong and she is getting better by the hour.

5:11 PM Jean has had a good day, resting, eating a little, sleeping a bit more. Her chest drains are out and this has lessened some of the discomfort she had this morning. She was able to sit in a chair for a short time, but was not ready yet to walk about. Her sister, Barbara and her husband John were here too so Jean got to visit with them for a few minutes each time they were allowed in to see her. Security is not airtight but the nurses do control the admission of people so that they can keep Jean safe and so she doesn't wear herself out. She is so social that she would keep cheering and greeting people without regard for her own rest. I hope she will one day realize that she has to be as concerned for her own welfare as she is for others. I know she is getting stronger as she has given me a 'honey do' list for tomorrow, things she wants me to bring to her. Amy and I will leave shortly so that Jean can rest the night without having to be serving others from her heart.

8:56 PM I spoke with Donna, Jean's night nurse, just now and she reported that Jean is sleeping, finally and well I hope. She has really struggled to sleep soundly for weeks now and so I hope this means that she is finally getting the deep, restful sleep she craves. Tomorrow brings us one day closer to ending the "critical" period that follows the trauma of such significant invasive surgery as this. She has been through a terrible and ghastly invasion of her chest and is just now beginning to see the results full force. Since that first night the difference is so marked it is startling as I am *the only one who saw her that first night and believe me it was not an easy thing to comprehend. But just these few hours and days since, she has rebounded so well that it is surreal as Amy described it today. I hate to rush the passage of time, but I wish for the days to race by so we can see what this all means quickly and know the full impact and effect of her transplant. I am prone to impatience anyway, so this is exceedingly hard to wait for the results to be seen and understood. But, I will have no choice.*

11/4/07 5:15 AM DAY 3 I spoke with Donna, Jean's night nurse and was informed that Jean had a good night's sleep. Pain meds seemed to be helping her more too. Oxycodone was prescribed and Jean was able to continue sleeping. The more she sleeps, the sooner she will heal and the better pain relief will be.

6:48 PM Well, Jean had a mixed kind of day today. Her heart continues to be fine, but she struggled with lung function and some breathlessness necessitating more oxygen inhalation to assist her lungs to expand more fully. She has been breathing too shallowly for so long that the lower rear lobes of her lungs have not been doing all they can. While on the Bi Pac machine her oxygen levels hit 100% immediately but as soon as the inhalation staff took her off the Bi Pac and on to the mask or cannula, her oxygen levels dropped to around 84-85. The doctors think this is just an adjustment issue and are confident they can handle it as a fine-tuning matter. They did call in pulmonology and in case Jean needs it, they have an alert in to the dialysis team, although her kidney function seems to be okay. They just want to be sure. Due to the fact that Jean became breathless so easily, the nurse decided not to have Jean walk today although she did sit up for a brief period. It felt like a setback day to us because we have come to see such dramatic improvement that we expected it would continue to be so, but today reminded us that we have to patient and let things adjust, as they will. Amy left to return to CO in the late afternoon and I decided to let Jean rest so I left around 5:30 as she was trying to sleep. Last night, Jean said he had a good night's sleep and so I thought that leaving her to get another good night's sleep made sense. She still tires pretty easily.

11/5/07 DAY 4 Jean began walking today and is making great progress despite needing oxygen to get her lungs functioning at their peak. Medication adjustments are underway as a part of the reality of transplantation. Jean's body is making many adjustments all at the same time. When I visited her today, she was walking the halls and trying to clear her lungs as best she could. Later in the day, she walked a second time and then spent the rest of our time in her chair. I watched her eat a really good dinner, and she has gotten her appetite back so that is a very good sign. The heart and the systems that support it are working really well. The only issue remains her ability to breathe on her own, but the medical staff believe that that will come around shortly. So, today's challenge is to get through this day and face tomorrow.

11/6/07 DAY 5 Jean was able to walk the entire length and circumnavigate around the nurse's station this morning, using a cart as support and her oxygen level afterwards was very strong. It took her no time to get it back to 100% using an assist from her oxygen mask. So, the next step is for her to make that same circuit again today, and eventually, to do it without oxygen. The long process of rehabbing has begun in small ways. But she is getting physically stronger by the hour it seems.

11/7/07 DAY 6 Jean had a great night last night, sleeping the best since coming out of surgery. She is scheduled to walk again today. Last night she slept without the oxygen mask for the first time although still using the cannula. Today, our son, Joe, is arriving from Denver and I will be leaving shortly to pick him up at Bradley and going straight to the hospital for his first visit. Keep the vigil going, as there is still a far distance to go. God knows what is around the next corner, and He isn't sharing that information with us ahead of time.

Our son Joe arrived at Yale around 4:45 today after his flight from Denver. The reunion was very special. Jean was sitting in bed without oxygen for the first time since the transplant. She told us that she is being moved Friday to the step down unit where rehab will begin. Today, she walked the unit, had many of the IVs taken out. Tomorrow, the rest of her IVs will be pulled; her catheter will also be pulled in preparation for leaving for the rehab unit. Her nurse, Maila, told us that of all the transplant patients she has had she would rate Jean as the second fastest to recover! How's that for setting a record? Her progress has been nothing short of spectacular and if she continues to progress at the current rate, she will be home as early as next Wednesday! Of course, we are thrilled about the prospect of that, but will remain cautious in case any last minute changes pop up. Jean has to get used to the idea that she no longer has heart disease. She hesitated to order chocolate ice cream, but when she called it in, she was greeted with an okay and soon was eating her first chocolate ice cream in quite a long time. Even her salt intake is no longer an issue. Once she gets whatever dietary instructions there may be, I think she is going to be surprised to know that she can eat normally again. Her new heart is healthy and her diet will reflect that change. Jean no longer has heart disease! Trying to get your head around that idea is so foreign after all the years she was restricted in so many ways. It continues to amaze me how well she looks and how strong she is. Simply amazing. The doctors and nurses have been so encouraging, even mentioning that traveling in the next year or so will no longer be a problem if Jean continues to move in the direction she now seems to be headed. The miracle keeps getting better each day.

Josh Groban and Charlotte Church (among others, including Andrea Bocelli) have captured the sense of things through today in their rendition of the song, The Prayer. *Our, and your many, prayers have been answered so I offer you this as way to show our appreciation to you and the Almighty who has made all this possible. We are never alone when we have our faith, our family and our friends. We pray for continued strength and in thanksgiving for all you have meant to us in our trials helping Jean to make it this far so fast. David Foster and Carol Bayer Sager wrote the words and music for this song. It was originally written for the animated film,* Quest for Camelot: *"I pray you'll be our eyes … And watch us where we go … And help us to be wise … In times when we don't know … Let this be our prayer … When we lose our way … Lead us to a place … Guide us with your grace … To a place where we'll be safe … I pray we'll find your light … And hold it in our hearts … When stars go out each night … Guide us with your grace … Give us faith so we'll be safe … We ask that life be kind … And watch us from above … We hope each soul will find … Another soul to love."*

11/8/07 DAY 7 All tubes have been removed. Jean is disconnected from oxygen and breathing on her own. She is ambulatory although still fairly weak and easily fatigued. But she is making miraculous progress to say the least. It has not yet been a full week post-transplant! And, yet she is already so much stronger and better than before. You will not believe her color and how vibrant she looks now that her heart is functioning so well. Last night she ate chocolate ice cream; who knows what today will bring? Son Joe is with her while I continue to teach so she has company. Daughter Stacie is making plans to travel back here again next week to be home with Jean when she arrives so we have our own private duty nurse right in the family. Daughter Amy will return in early December too to once again assist us in the medications compliance Jean will need to follow. We already know that Jean will be unable to drive for a few months until her sternum is completely healed, so she will be dependent on family and friends to get places, but I know she'll welcome just the ability to move around without being tethered to lines and machines. She may have to reprise the role from Driving Miss Daisy so as to avoid airbag deployment by taking the backseat! Oh my God, that means she will really be my backseat driver! I will have to be on my toes or I'll hear about it. But I will be thrilled just to have in the car with me again. Each week for the first month, starting next Tuesday, Jean will be brought in for outpatient biopsy of the heart to detect any signs of rejection. In the second month every two weeks and then, if all goes well, every month for the remainder of the year. If rejection is controlled and fine-tuned enough with immunosuppressant medications, Jean will need a biopsy once a year or only if something else triggers a need for one. Doctors have already told Jean and me that travel we have postponed can once again be planned once this next year passes and so maybe we can get to do the things we wanted to do when "we got older" sooner rather than never. Jean's health has for the past few years been a significant concern whenever we traveled or planned to go somewhere. Now, maybe Italy and Greece may be in our sights.

11/9/07 DAY 8 Some time this morning Jean will be transferred to 4 - 7 in the East Pavilion where she will begin her PT/OT and other cardiac rehab work to get her back to full strength. We will learn all the exercises and limitations she will have as well as what expectations we will have for her return to full functioning and the timelines for some activities. We have already been told that Jean will not be able to drive for a few months so that her sternum will not be exposed to possible impact with a steering wheel in case of an accident. It is unclear whether she will be able to be in the front seat exposed to possible airbag deployment or whether she must ride in the rear seat, but we're hoping that she'll be able to ride up front. Questions like these and others will be answered here. And so, we begin again to rebuild Jean's health now that she no longer has heart disease. It would something to behold if she returned to her former self when she would come home from Curves and show off her biceps with that little girl smile on her face that always made me laugh with joy knowing she was "pumping iron." I'd kid her to try the 5 lb weights next week.

Last evening, George, himself three years past his transplant on November 6, came to visit. He was simply amazed, his words, at Jean's meteoric progress. He was in a coma for days following his transplant. He commented on how different she looked from when he last saw her on 5 - 1 before her transplant and how she looked now. These positive comments boost my spirits as I hope that I am not looking at Jean with wishful thinking, but when I hear from nurse Maila Alvarez that Jean is the second fastest to recover that she has ever seen and then hear what George has to say, it validates my own impressions that she is remarkably, noticeably and refreshingly better already. Now, Jean has to hear and synthesize those sentiments herself to believe the miracle as others see it. I think she is beginning to understand but I have to keep reminding myself that things are different for her as she is viewing all of this from inside the experience while I, and others, view it from different perspectives, either subjectively, as in my case, or objectively, as in the case of the medical staff, nurses, and people like George, who themselves have seen if from inside. Why, when I think that Jean hasn't even recently read the website, I catch myself that we have all had much more awareness of everything, even the actual surgery itself, then Jean has. She was unconscious much of the time and has not been in front of a computer to read what has happened. So, in a very real and profound sense, she has missed so much! Yet, it is she who is at the center of it all. How different it must be for her.

Jean was not able to move out of CTICU today simply because there was no room available to her on 4 - 7. She must have a private room to avoid contact with other patients who might have any infections as she is under immunosuppressant drug therapy, which has weakened her immune system so that she cannot as easily fight off opportunistic infections. But, tomorrow, she is probably going to be able to move out then begin the next phase of rehab and exercise to get her home. She looks wonderful and is again talking on the phone, feeling fine and walking about as if she is brand new. Today, she walked without the aid of a cart and felt more natural doing this. Our son Joe and I visited with her most of the afternoon and early evening and she was awake and alert taking calls and teasing me, all good signs! Daughter Stacie is coming back on Tuesday to attend the discharge meeting and will be able to assist Jean's homecoming on Wednesday so we feel pretty secure that her transition will be smooth as silk.

11/10/07 DAY 9 Jean is getting even more home sick and impatient to leave now that she feels so good. Although she no longer needs the ICU, there is no free bed for her to transfer to and so we sit waiting and she is bored silly wanting to get on with things. She is isolated since there are no "friends" on this floor. Everyone here is pretty ill and restricted to bed by and large, except Jean. So, while she was able to socialize when she was on 5 - 1, here she can't get to know anyone. So, unless the boys and I are here, she has no one to talk to or visit with. Hopefully, the time will go quickly today and tomorrow so maybe she can be transferred to the new unit soon so that by Wednesday, she can leave for good.

Today, Jean got the chance to read the website for herself for the first time since before her transplant. I watched her as she reacted to what she was reading. She teared up a little now and then but I know she knows how much I love her. We pledged to never fail to tell each other each day that we loved each other and we made sure to tell our children each day and at every opportunity. She broke down a little too when she read the events of the day. She was never aware of the day after about 11:30 AM, so for her this was the first time she could see the day unfold and be a part of it even though she was at the center of it. She just looked over at me as I am writing this in her room and said, "Do your stuff!" That is her way of deflecting my attention from her as she reacts to the reading of the website. I think she is ready for this and so I printed a hard copy for her to peruse. It was very hard to leave Jean; as we departed she was crying softly and my heart sank but I know she is only sad because she can't come with us. I reminded her that she needed to put in only 72 more hours before she could leave for home. But still it hurts her to be left behind. That is the worst part of being hospitalized; you can't go when you want to leave. Your fate is in the hands of others. Wednesday cannot come soon enough for all of us, but especially for Jean. Stacie arrives Tuesday so she can attend the discharge meeting and be informed of the immediate after-care once Jean gets home. Joe departs the same day although later that day. He has been great to have around, as always, joking and laughing bringing joy to us all as he has always done.

11/11/07 DAY 10 It is Sunday morning, early, usually the time we would be getting up and deciding what to do today. I know that next week at this time, Jean will be here at home and we can have that conversation right here in the family room while we read the paper and look at the sales flyers. I am actually looking forward to discussing sales! That is a bit disconcerting but I'll enjoy it because Jean will be here with me. Usually, I would be looking at the sports page to see which football games I'd like to watch. I have been saying that we have a new normal. In a few days, I'll know better what that entails. I am excited to be this close to having Jean home again, but also a bit anxious about what it will be like after nearly 8 weeks of being a bachelor. For the first time in my adult life, my sons and I have been out sitting at a bar or restaurant having a dinner and drinks like three old friends. I have so enjoyed their camaraderie and will always relish the memory that we have been able to share these wonderful times in a way that would never have been possible because of distance and other circumstances in a time of great duress. Chris has been here all along and has been rock solid throughout. I am very proud of him and would welcome him in my foxhole any time. Joe, who had to come from Denver, has brought all of us his joyfulness and playfulness to lift all our spirits, and he too is a member of my foxhole team. Fathers have a different kind of love and emotion for their sons. I am blessed to have two men I admire for their love and warmth, their toughness and resilience and their understanding of their mother and father as people, not just as parents. I am profoundly proud of all my children, and these past few weeks have made me appreciate all of them again, in more adult and lasting ways, as each has played such an important part in this drama of life surrounding their mother, my love. They have saved their father great stress and angst simply by being here and being themselves. And, they always revert to their roles in the family. Joe, eldest son, the joyful playful one keeping everyone loose and relaxed; Chris the strong and powerful one being there by my side day after day and especially the day of the transplant; Stacie, the oldest daughter and nurse-in-charge working with the nurses to care for her mother; Amy, the pharmacist and professional instructor on proper use of medicines and inquiring about treatment staff on her mother's care. It all came together and with all the prayers and support from so many people, this has been quite a remarkable series of emotional swings.

11/12/07 DAY 11 Jean finally moved from CTICU at 2:30 AM today. I still don't know how this occurred so late in the night, but she is now on 4 and I will see her in her new room later this morning. She called me about 8:15 AM sounding tired from the night's ordeal of packing and moving during the wee hours. I guess she didn't get much sleep. It seems so strange to me that a hospital would take steps like this in the middle of the night when someone is recovering form transplant surgery. But, as close as we are to getting her home, I won't complain too strenuously. Jean and I spoke about the future of the website yesterday. She thinks that once she is home we ought to shut it down. I agree that this makes sense, as she will be home, able to call and visit her many friends and be mobile enough to get to the places and events she wants to see. So, we shall see. We're this close to having her home and putting this life-altering experience behind us where we can gain the perspective of distance and time that will permit us the chance to evaluate what has just happened to us all. We received a very generous call from Mary Charlton of FCCOL asking if we would need help with dinners, etc. after Jean got home. While we are touched by this generous offer, we ask that everyone be patient since we do not yet know fully what dietary restrictions Jean may have or whether she will have any other adjustments to make once she is home. I want to be certain that Jean is comfortable being home and has her bearings before we commit to anything that may cause her to feel the need to extend herself to visitors, friends, dinner offers, or anything else for that matter. Once we know where she stands in regards to being home, we will let church members and friends know how and when to visit her and to make good on all the wonderful gestures of support. I don't want her to *feel overwhelmed by the pressure of being "up" until she is sure is ready for all that goes along with that. She is strong and resilient, but I expect that her coming home will be quite emotional after nearly 8 weeks away. Thank you for understanding my wish to protect her a little bit until she is fully ready to move on.*

2 PM I called Jean after class to see how she was settling into 4 - 7 and she gave me the great news that Dr. Botta came by and told her she could go home Tuesday, not Wednesday! So, the blessings keep a-coming! I am on my way there now to see her for the afternoon and early evening. But, I will have to go home and pack clothes for her now that winter is here; she was admitted when it was still Indian summer! Imagine, she is almost home.

By 4:30 PM there was some uncertainty about Jean's leaving Tuesday, but Wednesday was seen as more definitive in case the biopsy was done on schedule Tuesday. Dr. Botta was being optimistic without having coordinated with the other members of the transplant team who have paperwork to complete for medications and other things and meetings to set up for discharge.   In a late day decision by Noreen Gorham the transplant nurse there was a slim chance that if the biopsy was done early in the morning, and the results could be determined quickly, there was a chance that Jean could leave Tuesday afternoon or early evening. If not, then Wednesday for sure, she can come home.

11/13/07 DAY 12 7:13 AM Stacie is en route via CT Limo directly to Yale from Bradley. Joe and I will shortly be leaving to join her there in anticipation that Jean will be discharged either today or tomorrow. Today, she gets her first biopsy on her heart and we will know the status of rejection activity. Those results determine the way medications are adjusted to fend off rejection, which is and will be the main issue for Jean's recovery from this point forward. The biopsy is scheduled at 7:30 AM and is actually scheduled as an outpatient test so that gets Jean into the queue as this will be a weekly test for the next month, then every two weeks, then monthly through the first year.

8:50 PM We left Jean in good spirits at the end of a very long day. We were educated about the medications and other issues that Jean now faces. She could have left today but due to delays in the biopsy schedule because of flight for life incoming patients. We are confident that the future is bright and that Jean will begin her rehabilitation in earnest with VNA and cardiac rehab over the next few months. Her weight is down to 119 lbs and she shows some atrophy but that is expected after being so long confined to bed and just now being able to ambulate and move. Starting tomorrow she will be back on familiar turf and we fully expect her to regain her strength and full muscle tone as soon as she begins to do more. The discharge team remarked how well she has responded and they fully expect that she will continue to make great strides. On another good news level, Jean's friend, Frenchie, whom she met at the CICU got her new heart last night and she actually replaced Jean in the same room Jean recovered from her own transplant surgery on CTICU. We could not be happier that Frenchie too got her new heart so that she and Jean will be cohorts in the follow up and support group meetings to come. They will be seeing each other at biopsy appointments and other affairs. So, the miracle of transplantation has made two families happy that there were people so committed to helping others. We, and Frenchie's family, now know how vitally important donation can be to so many.

Chapter 3 - Starting Over at Home

11/14/07 DAY 13 This is the best day of all so far. After just 13 days, Jean is coming home with her new heart! God has been good to us at a time of tragedy for another family, ours has been deemed worthy of another chance at new life. The magnitude of this has not been lost on any of us. We realize painfully how the loving and yet agonizing gesture of strangers has made Jean's return from death's door possible. We will never take that for granted. Once again, we ask that you think about donation. Only 2000 people a year get the gift that Jean has gotten. That number has not changed for many years. People are dying waiting for organs that never come simply because others do not give, are not aware or simply never thought of what they might be able to do for others. We urge all who read this, please talk about donation to everyone you know. As we head into what will be our best Thanksgiving ever, we ask that when thanking God for your blessings, you think about how this gift that Jean has had given her could be replicated by millions of others who might be able to make the same thing possible for others who are gravely ill. Check your driver's license to see if you are a donor, if you are, great; but if you are not, then please reconsider becoming a donor. It is very personal to us. Maybe, we can together save others' lives by simply being generous in our deaths so that we give back life when we are given that opportunity. There is no greater love.

11:00 AM Jean exited Yale at about 11:00 AM. I took her picture while she waited to get in the Beetle to be driven home by Stacie so I could get to the university to teach. On their way home, they stopped for Jean's first lunch out of the hospital since September. So, Jean is back among us and eating food that she likes. Tonight we will be home together enjoying our peace and tranquility. I will count this as DAY 1 HOME.

11/15/07 DAY 2 AT HOME Jean enjoyed being home with family. Last night she was able to sleep in her own bed for the first time in months. Our special meal together, can you guess, was pizza! Of course. Although she was up a few times during the night, I could tell that she was settling in again. Alia made a welcome home banner with hand painted hearts all over it; Marge from FCCOL sent a magnificent basket of flowers that adorn the dining room table. Alia and Chris decorated the house with balloons so there was a festive welcome home. Last night, Stacie arranged the medications according to specific requirements that Jean has to follow very closely. The cocktail of medications is designed to keep Jean's heart working without the threat of rejection episodes so it is highly prescriptive and must be rigidly followed every single day. This morning the kids each went in to see Jean asking the ineluctable question, "How'd you sleep mom?" Although Chris calls her mama in his variation of the question. Today will be Jean's first full day here at home. So now we will see how she responds to the rigorous weigh-ins, temps, bps and heart rates we have to take during the day. We're ready.

Jean continues to labor with her stamina not being so great yet. Understandably, her body is weakened by her long hospital stay and the trauma to her body. She tires very easily and even little things like getting up and moving to another chair or room takes a lot of energy. VNA is coming by today to assist and to offer some PT support. Soon, we hope Jean will regain some lost muscle mass and begin to feel better. Her heart is strong even if she is not yet back to her old level of stamina. She is being cared for by all of us so that we must be cognizant of the reality of balancing her need with getting around on her own and knowing when to rest. This will take time, but we will get her going on her own pace as she feels better and better. Each day we hope to see improvement as she re-acclimates to the demands of being home and on her own turf. Her weight is the lowest it has been since I first met her as a young woman in 1965. Ben & Jerry's might help!

A little spike in BP today but a prescription was filled to get this under control right away. This is not at all unusual in transplantation but we will be vigilant in monitoring. Jean spent today putting the house back in order and tried to run Stacie out of the kitchen. Stacie prevailed and made dinner, baking some muffins and a cake to try to fatten Jean up. Tonight, we will enjoy a homemade meal for the first time in quite a while. It's good to have family here to ease the load. Jean needs to rest more than she ever has been asked to before. She will never like it but she will have to get used to it and accept her limitations for this period of time. One day soon, she will be back rattling the pots and pans. Baking is another issue altogether; Jean never enjoyed that. Just as well, as I don't need that to make me fat. I don't need any help at all.

11/16/07 DAY 3 AT HOME A much better night last night than the previous night. Jean's BP this morning was great having had only one dose of BP medication at bedtime last night, so that seems to be correcting well already. Stamina is still a matter of concern as she tires so easily, but we are going to try to get her out of the house a little bit today and see if that'll help perk her up. Maybe a lunch date will help. We shall see what the day brings. Jean went out to the grocery store today, shopping for food with Stacie. She was out about an hour and enjoyed the fresh, crisp November air. Friend Arnie Mann called, as did Jean's sister Barbara and her aunt, Sister Rita. Jean did not talk much on the phone as she still finds it tiring a bit, but she is doing her breathing exercises and has been able to sustain the Spirometer test a few seconds each breath. We had Chinese food for the first time in quite a while now that Jean can eat more seasoned food for the first time in years. Our backyard neighbor, Shawna Turner, brought over a welcome home balloon and a lovely vase of flowers, too, a gift from husband Zack, Bella the dog and Bailey the cat. Made the Chinese dinner a bit more formal.

11/17/07 DAY 4 AT HOME BP and pulse again were solid but no weight gain change yet. Jean is eating well but her weight gain has been negligible so far. Stacie makes her eat breakfast, lunch and dinner and is trying to get her to eat 5 small meals a day as a way to gain some muscle. I have never had that problem! If I pass by food, I absorb its calorie content by osmosis. But I would not want to endure what Jean has to lose weight. Weight Watchers is hard enough for me. Today, we hope to get Jean out again for more air and exercise.

We had a busy day taking Jean out for lunch at Cafe Tuscana in Old Saybrook, then a short road trip to Wal-Mart to see Alia, then Best Buy, although she stayed in the car with Stacie while Chris and I returned a printer that wouldn't work. We had a visit from Glenn Miele, who tried in vain with me to get the new wireless printer to work. After two days of trying even with Glenn's expertise (he works for HP who manufactured the printer!) we could not get it to work. So, we brought it back and we had a reason to take Jean out for some fresh air and a ride. It was not a "top down" kind of day so we took the 4Runner and all rode together like the family we used to be, less two of the kids. Jean ate a hearty lunch of soup and piece of Stacie's eggplant panini. Her appetite is definitely showing improvement. Cards keep coming from friends and family too so we know that lots of people are keeping Jean in their thoughts and prayers. Our neighbors, Terry and Luann, brought a magnificent fruit basket for Jean and the family. We were delighted by their wonderful generosity and gesture of neighborliness.

11/18/07 DAY 5 AT HOME VNA is sending out a nurse this morning to check on Jean. This will continue briefly until we think she is off and running toward full recovery. Stacie and I discussed the possibility of giving back to the organ donation program in the nation by possible publication of this website as a fund raising and/or awareness raising opportunity. We even tossed around ideas for a title, The Heart of the Matter, Straight to the Heart, were ideas we came up while sitting here waiting for the nurse to arrive. She just knocked on the door. VNA stayed for about an hour taking vitals and answering questions with Jean. We requested physical therapy as soon as possible to avert any more tumbles and to get Jean stronger as quickly as possible. Maybe with a little professional attention that will speed things along a bit better. Plans today include dinner at Anthony's in Guilford, one of Jean's favorite places to eat. See, her appetite is better and her weight today was up another pound! Good signs all around and she is beginning to grouse about the house being, using her words, "a mess", which means that she is noticing some things out of place. I never thought I'd be pleased to hear her complaining about such things, but I am making exceptions this time around. We even purged the fridge today. So, the boss is back! Oddly, if there is a mess, it is much of the stuff we need for her care that is around the house. I even vacuumed today right in front of her to prove my manhood! I'm sure glad I bought the new light weight Oreck that weighs less than 5 lbs for Jean before she went into the hospital, proves how smart I am. Now, I get to use it. Hmmm! I grow suspicious of her motives.

11/19/07 DAY 6 AT HOME Jean's pain level has not decreased much yet and it really tires her out, so we were able to get her a prescription for pain relief. She was, at first, reluctant to take the meds, but last night she finally conceded and she got her first full, uninterrupted night's sleep since she came home. I woke her early since I had to leave for a one-day conference that required me to meet a colleague at 7:30 AM. We planned ahead so that I could have Jean ready, showered and have the vital signs done, the meds set up and be able to feel reasonably sure that she was safe. Stacie left on the red-eye back to CO very early this morning, Chris getting up at 3:30 AM to drive her to Bradley before he went to work, Alia was off today so we knew that by mid-morning Jean would be with someone and that I would be home early in the afternoon so that she would not be alone. I got home around 1:15. Jean and I went shopping for a ride to get her out of the house for just a little bit. She tired pretty quickly so we came back shortly thereafter. She is now resting and enjoying the King of Queens, and I am going to join her. Stacie, Jean and I, last evening, arranged her meds for the coming week; we color coded the array of meds so that we can keep track of what and when. Tomorrow, Jean has her second biopsy and blood draw so we may see a reduction in the meds; two have already been discontinued so we keep hoping for more to come out of the regimen as she makes progress.

11/20/07 DAY 7 AT HOME Today started Jean's outpatient status for follow-up procedures. We were at 800 Howard at 7:30 AM for blood draw, then over to the hospital for her first heart biopsy that was scheduled for an unspecified time and did not occur until 9:45 when she went down to have it done. She was back up on 4 by around 11:20 and was discharged around 1:20. We now know what to expect in this new phase. This will be the routine for the next three weeks. Then the schedule moves to every two weeks. We just received the fist biopsy results and the news is great -- no sign of rejection! So, we will have more good news to celebrate Thursday, Thanksgiving day.

11/21/07 DAY 8 AT HOME Jean is resting today after yesterday's ordeal. The biopsy is pretty painful and done without anesthesia so she is a bit sore and stiff today; after all, her heart was pierced microscopically so that the doctors can see if there is any T4 cell activity in the tissue of the heart that would indicate rejection activity is at work. Happily there are none as I reported last evening. VNA came again today and, on Friday, PT will start as well. After her discharge yesterday, Jean went back to CICU where she resided for 6 weeks and presented the nurses there with some gifts of thanks. (We wanted to visit Frenchie but were told she was going in for another procedure so we will wait till next week, when she and Jean will meet again in the pre-biopsy room on 4.) While there, she and I were introduced to a young man named Tony, who was admitted the very day Jean received her new heart. He heard all the hubbub and has asked every day, "how's Jean?". Kendra, Jean's nurse, asked Jean if she would mind meeting Tony, and of course she never hesitated to visit him. I was so proud to watch her and to listen to her giving a complete stranger her support and advice about how to prepare himself for what only she and other transplanted human beings can relate to. She was so sweet and kind to him, just as she is with all people she meets. I can see her being quite the activist one day, taking on the issue of transplant advocacy and support group work as a way to give back. Jean was amazing. Calm, poised and confident standing bedside and delivering her "best Jean has to offer" advice. I was ready to donate my heart if I could have to help Tony, but obviously that can't be done. We all have to think about how we can leave the legacy of healing others when it is our turn to donate.

11/22/07 DAY 9 AT HOME The day began with the usual start up events of weight, BP, pulse and meds. Jean is gaining weight, which, for the first time in her life, is a good thing! (Don't we all wish we could use more weight?) She needs to regain the loss of muscle mass she has had due to atrophy from lengthy hospitalization. Today Jean's weight was up so we are delighted to see that. She has a bit of a headache and some congestion in her head, but we don't think this is anything to be too concerned about except that her immune system is suppressed by the meds and so any sign of fever is a concern. No fever was evident this morning when I took her vitals. Yesterday, late, we were called by the transplant team staff and were advised to lower the med level on one of the immune suppressants, which is a good sign, based on Jean's biopsy result. We think that this means that the heart is doing well and rejection is not at this time a factor to be worried about. Of course, rejection is going to be a lifelong concern but we'll take the one-day-at-a-time approach on this. Each day is a miracle. Happy Thanksgiving everyone.

Jean has been resting all day. She is more tired than usual although her headache has subsided. She seemed pretty subdued at dinner, deep in thought and quiet. She led the prayer before we ate and I suspect that she was pretty overwhelmed by all that has transpired these past few weeks. I know she is emotionally over-wrought at times so we will be patient and watch for her to rebound soon. Tomorrow, the

VNA PT arrives to start Jean's rehab. I certainly hope she is up to the challenge so she can gain some strength and begin to feel like herself -- whatever that means since we do not know what feeling good will translate into because for so long she has not felt good at all. Calls came from family, friends and FCCOL members. Our son-in-law, Andy, has introduced us to Skype, an Internet on-camera phone service where we can see the grandkids live and talk to them over the Internet using our laptop camera. It is amazing what we can do with these things to stay in touch in real time with live video feeds. It took several tries but we got it to work on both ends. Too bad that by the time we got both ends working Jean was napping, but we'll get her on later so she can see our grandsons in CO along with their parents, assorted aunts and uncles, who all met at Stacie's home for dinner.

11/23/07 DAY 10 AT HOME Jean is still in bed as I write this. She was very tired yesterday, even napping during the day a bit, which is highly unusual for her. So, I think she was feeling weak and needed to rest more than usual. Today the first visit from the PT is scheduled and we will see how that goes. I hope to be here when the PT arrives although I have an early appointment to get the car serviced so that I can participate and be made aware of the various activities Jean will need to engage in order to get back to full strength.

10 AM Jean continues to run a fever so I have called Yale to see what we need to do. If she continues to have fever and it goes past 100, I have to get her to Yale's ER ASAP. So, today is our first "not so good" day of after-care experience. PT is scheduled for 1 PM but likely will be less than useful unless Jean rebounds and feels better by then. I may have to cancel that if we are leaving for ER.

3 PM Jean has rested all day and her fever has diminished to a safe level at around 98.8, so we have averted an ER visit today. But, she still is very lethargic and not feeling too terribly good, with lots of pain in her back and chest. It could be 6 months before she feels no pain, we're told, so we just have to fight through it and hope it improves day to day. We rescheduled PT for Sunday. By then, hopefully, Jean will be feeling a little better than she is now. Jean had a light lunch so I know her appetite is not great either, but that is probably a function of her feeling so bad. I will try to get her to eat a solid dinner with more protein.

11/24/07 DAY 11 AT HOME Jean awoke without fever after a good night's sleep. She ate breakfast after we took vitals and she is off to the start of the day. I just realized that today marks the 23rd day post transplant and is also the 42nd anniversary of the day Jean and I met at a fraternity party in Madison, NJ. I will forever be indebted to my fraternity brother, Brian Fallon, for bringing Jean and her friends to that party. Had he not, I would never have met Jean is my guess and the karmic magic that occurred that night would never have brought us together. Now, lo these many years later, we are still together, but there will be no party tonight! That's okay, we are together and that is what matters most of all.

PM Prepped the meds box today for the coming week. Jean has 18 meds in the AM and 10 in the PM; some are scheduled for both, but some are just once a day. They range widely in color and size from tiny to horse pill! She has to swallow them all. God bless her. I couldn't imagine doing this, but I guess if my life depended on swallowing these I would have little choice but to do so. And, she is actually reducing some of the meds, as they are faded based on blood and biopsy results. At some point, Jean will likely and happily be taking just the minimal number and minimal doses necessary to assure rejection is controlled. Now, we're off to see what's for dinner! Calzone with spinach and onions, yummy.

11/25/07 DAY 12 AT HOME I am up early and waiting for Jean to signal that she too is ready to start her day. I prepare her meds, get the vital equipment and notebook out, start her breakfast preparation so she can get the day off on the right foot. Jean was never a big breakfast eater before but now with all the meds she has to take, she really must eat so that she can get these pills down and keep them down. So, I am off to the kitchen.

Jean has had a comfortable morning. She ate well, did very well in her VNA visit and is now awaiting the arrival of the PT this afternoon. This will be critically important to her revitalization and rehabilitation so that she can get up and be moving better as her strength is still subpar. Her weight is getting better but that must be converted to muscle strength so she is more mobile, more independent and able to feel confident that she can do what she wants to do. I know she wants to get back in the kitchen and she misses work badly, missing her friends there and wanting to be around those she enjoys. She was pretty emotional the other day when Bob called from the FCCOL to wish her a Happy Thanksgiving. The gesture was appreciated but it left her feeling even more acutely how much she misses work. The holidays are always the busiest time of the year at a church so she knows what she is missing. But work is still a ways off and remains to be seen whether that can really occur at all. Building back her strength will be vital in all that happening one day, so she sure has the necessary motivation and a goal to work towards. I guess we will be home watching some football, not Jean, but I will surely be as both the Giants and the Broncos are on back-to-back today. Life is good!

PT Heidi has given Jean a nice set of exercises to do while seated, made suggestions for raising the toilet seat so egress is easier. We cut down a cane to fit Jean's height and she was instructed in ways to get out of bed easier so that she does not need to use her shoulders and chest muscles too vigorously. All in all, Jean is in better shape than she thinks for all she's been through and Heidi confirmed that to her. I think that made Jean feel better too. Plus, getting pain relief without Vicodin has made her more alert and more able to get around more safely and more steadily on her feet.

11/26/07 DAY 13 AT HOME Jean spent her first day sort of alone. I went back to the university for the first time since she came home and without back up at home. She as feeling pretty spry today as I found her wandering around the house when I called mid-morning to see how she was, she told she was in the dining room straightening things up a little. That's code for, "the house is a mess" and therefore not up to her standards of the perfect house. You gotta love her spunk. I will see how the rest of the day really went when I get home later this afternoon. Alia was at home today so there was someone there for part of the time. Her sister arrived just in time for dinner armed with veal and peppers, one of Jean's favorites. Tuesday is my long and late day, so I will be glad to have someone with her so she isn't too lonely sitting at home. Once the semester is over, just before Christmas, I will be around everyday until the spring semester begins in late January so Jean'll hardly ever be alone for the weeks in the interim. I think that is a good thing, but she'll be the judge of that I suppose! Tomorrow Jean goes for her third biopsy and I know she is anticipating that with some dread as it is very painful to endure and there is little anesthesia used in the procedure. Plus, I will not be there for this one to keep her company, as our friend Aimee Miele is going to help Jean tomorrow. Once she is home, I will feel better. Tuesdays will be the day we will not look forward to as long as Jean is getting these biopsies but that is the nature of this; there is a lot of ambivalence. You always have to keep an eye on rejection episodes but the biopsies are invasive and painful, but essential. Next month, if all goes well, they will be done every two weeks so they'll be spaced out more but still cause for dread. Jean is having a very nice visit with her sister and her spirits are appreciably better as a result. I think the distraction will help her to keep her mind off tomorrow's events as long as possible. Tonight we packed the bag we take to Yale with her morning meds, which she takes after the blood draw but before the biopsy along with the binder where we record all the vitals and monitor meds.

11/27/07 DAY 14 AT HOME Jean's biopsy is done and she is having lunch at 12:50 at Yale waiting for her next appointment. She had an interesting morning already with blood draw delayed due to computer problems, then a tumble getting out of the building and back in the car to go over for the biopsy, then going through another biopsy. She did get to meet up with her friend Frenchie while they were waiting for their biopsies. Unfortunately for me, I was unable to see her, as I would have liked. Maybe another time. Now, we wait for the biopsy results that tell us how well the heart is doing vis-à-vis rejection so that any meds that need adjusting can be adjusted accordingly. Tonight is a late night for me so I won't get to see Jean until around 11 PM so I hope to find her in good spirits having faced this day with her usual anxiety about the ordeal. Each time she goes through this, I shudder and hope she will find it less arduous but know that she feels fear about the whole experience. I certainly can't blame her for that, after all, they are invading her heart with a probe snaked down through her neck! It hurts just writing that. Aimee Miele may never recover from her day as Jean's tour guide for the day! They got lost, were late, Jean fell, they were late, Jean had to go for more tests, then another appointment. It was a whole day. Welcome to the world of transplant! Thanks, Aimee. We appreciate your dedicating a whole day to helping us out.

11/28/07 DAY 15 AT HOME Good news again today. Jean's biopsy was once again negative for rejection. Thank goodness for that. Medication changes were made to assist her uresis, which is rearing its head again in the form of some swelling in her ankles so the meds will go after that. Life Line equipment was installed today too; this helps Jean to get weighed, takes her BP, heart rate and oxygen levels just like when she was in the hospital. Then, it relays all that via phone to VNA where the data are tracked for any changes that warrant attention. This is high tech, computerized data collection via phone relayed to a computer and then interpreted by a cardiac trained nurse, Mary Allegra, nurse specialist at VNA who then translates it and works with Dr. Katz's office to keep Jean home and to avoid hospitalization. Another amazing bit of technology. We may be going out tonight to celebrate my birthday, but that will depend on how Jean recovers from her day at her favorite sporting event -- shopping! She tells me there is contact involved, so that makes it a sport. Right! I disagree strenuously, but what do I know? It may in fact be the biggest sports league in the world -- the WSL. Women's Shopping League. What? You thought, World Soccer League? Dinner treat at the Hideaway was Jean's first foray there since she came home. We were treated wonderfully warmly by Toni, Jack, Jeremy, Lori, Rich, Deb and Ken and Happy Birthday was sung by the patrons even though the candle was on the wrong dessert. Well meaning, just badly aimed. That didn't keep me from indulging in a decadent dessert. This is the oldest I've ever been.

11/29/07 DAY 16 AT HOME Jean is experiencing edema again which has us a bit perplexed so we are watching it with the doctors and VNA to see what may be causing this. We are closely monitoring to be sure it does not worsen. So, we are elevating her feet, using support hose and she's taking it easy. Meanwhile Jean reported that her pain is down to a level 4, which is the best she has reported since coming home. She is able to move about a bit better and is becoming a little more self-dependent, all good signs. Tomorrow, she has a urology consult, Monday, a transplant follow up, Tuesday support group holiday party/meeting. Other than that; not much going on.

11/30/07 DAY 17 AT HOME Today started out with a long telephone interview with Social Security so that Jean can apply for SSDI in the event she cannot return to work, although I know she very much would like to some day. Oddly, but I guess in self-defense, they tell you it will be months and months before you hear whether you're eligible, and even more months before you receive a single penny of benefits. They build in the discouragement to hold you off from beating down their door. In addition, they tell you that SSA turns over the determination of eligibility to the state of CT, who then asks you the same series of questions all over again! CT then determines and notifies SSA of its decision, then you appeal in the very unlikely event they approve you the first time. If you appeal, you have to comply with all sorts of deadlines and timelines you have to meet, but they don't have to, for speedy handling! That took the better part of an hour. If having a heart transplant is not a sufficient disabling condition, I will be very interested in hearing their reasons. We shall see. I had my annual physical today (always right around my birthday as a gift to myself), passing with flying colors, thankfully. I need to keep myself in shape in order to be able to assist Jean in whatever she has to do to be well. I am blessed with good genetics, my mother turned 93 in October and she still lives alone in FL, so I pray that I acquired her genetic predisposition for longevity and heartiness. My dad, too, was healthy right up until he acquired ALS in his late 70's, or I believe he would still be alive today. Barbara's husband, John, has just returned or the night and to take Barbara home to NJ tomorrow. So, we will have revolving visitors one again with Amy and her travel companion, Karen, who is on her way to Philly after stopping off here for a few days to visit Jean. Amy'll stay while Karen moves on. That'll give Jean and me some back up for next week's visits and support group activities so I can get to my classes and see the semester through to the end, which is fast approaching. Tonight we got a Skype call. For those of you not familiar with Skype, it is a computer based video and phone hook up where you can, for free, link your computer to another and by camera, see each other while you talk. It is the modern way to see and speak with grandkids who live far away. It's not like being able to hold them, but it is as good as you can get from 1500 miles away. Made our night. They got to visit their Groma, Aunt Barbara, Uncle John, Alia and Poppop all in one call.

12/1/07 DAY 18 AT HOME A new month starts and finds Jean still improving. Her weight went up again today, but there is concern that some of it is swelling due to fluid retention and the side effects of Prednisone. Monday, Jean visits the transplant team doctors so we hope to get a better handle on this recurring problem. Barbara and John depart today. They were gracious and Barbara took good care of the kitchen duties preparing meals that were healthy and voluminous. Jean's weight gain may have been affected by that "diet" as well. So, today we embark on another day of rehabbing, getting out for short "field trips" and hanging around the house.

12/2/07 DAY 19 AT HOME Jean had a restful night but awoke to considerable pain so we canceled our plans to get to church erring on the side of caution. We are just going to hunker down and be at home. The McCrackens are coming by this morning to visit. Jean will seek comfort in her favorite TV movie channel and the new batch of Godiva chocolate from our friend, Don Costello from my SARAH Inc. days. Good news, Jean's weight was down a couple of pounds indicating that her recent gain was just fluid retention, not related to chocolate intake and Anthony's Restaurant. Her stamina is creeping at an upward trend, but she is still weaker than we would like. PT is sporadic so we try to keep her moving as much as possible without stressing her too much. It is a delicate balance to say the least.

12/3/07 DAY 20 AT HOME Jean had her first post-operative meeting with Dr. Katz today. She has done beautifully and all signs look positive as we go forward. The only remaining issues are pain control but that will end when it ends. In the meantime, Jean is instructed to use pain relief medications. Today was a good day all around as Jean was out, shopped a little for food with Amy and I was able to meet up with them at Katz's office in time to be in attendance for the entire appointment after leaving the university.

12/4/07 DAY 21 AT HOME Biopsy day again. Amy is taking Jean to Yale today leaving very early due to the icy road conditions so she had time to spare. We fully expect the results again to be very good.

12/5/07 DAY 22 AT HOME As of this writing, there is still no word about yesterday's biopsy results, but we do not expect any problems, always remaining optimistic that Jean will be fine. Unfortunately, I came home yesterday with a fever and chills and had to be quarantined away from Jean so as to not subject her to any threat of infection. I went right to bed, awoke feeling a little better and went to work to teach and get some things done. I will feel better once I know what the biopsy report says. Jean did mention that it took her 6 hours last night to watch a movie because she had received so many phone calls that kept interrupting the video. She was exaggerating I know, but it is good for her to be socializing. I suspect that it would be better for her to receive calls during the early part of the day rather than at night when she is more fatigued. She continues to grow stronger day by day. Some meds were changed again reducing the steroids and increasing some others. Jean is now taking 22 meds in the morning and a smaller number at night.

12/6/07 DAY 23 AT HOME Jean is taking it easy today. VNA came this morning for a nursing visit with another PT visit tomorrow. Jean has dropped a few pounds, which is intentional. She reported that she is feeling stronger each day. I remain in quarantine still fighting a flu bug or something so I am trying to stay out of her way. Jean supervised the erecting of a new Christmas tree that will fit in our living room. We have never had a tree here in Old Lyme as we have spent every Christmas in Denver as our gift to ourselves so we could be with the kids and grandchildren. But, this year is different so we decided to put up a tree. Our old one is much too large to fit the room, so Amy went shopping for smaller tree we can use. It looks great and adds just enough cheer without overpowering the room. We even had some Christmas music playing while she worked.

12/7/07 DAY 24 AT HOME Early morning came the PT, Janice, working Jean's muscles groups for her legs, arms, chest and back. The surgery does a lot of damage across the ribs both in front and back as they are wrenched in a very unnatural way from their original direction stressing all the ligaments and tendons in the process. Working those back into their natural positions and back to their normal range of function and motion takes effort. In order to make the operating field large enough to remove the native heart and then place the donor heart the ribs are cracked along the sternum and opened wide forcing great strain on them especially in the back of the rib cage where the torque of the opening is felt. Jean has an appointment today for another consultation not directly related to her transplant but one we hope will help her shake a persistent problem with some potential for infection concerns. Amy will be taking her into New Haven one more time. Then, tonight in celebration of Amy's departure, we will go out for dinner and thank her for her yeoman efforts getting both of us through the week. She got more than she bargained for when I got sick Tuesday! Poor kid wound up doing all my stuff too. She came to care for her mother and got two for the price of one. Thank God for youth.

12/8/07 DAY 25 AT HOME The first measurable snowfall of the season came during the night. I awoke to see the yard white. My favorite time of year. I love snow. Now, however, that has to be tempered somewhat as I know this weather presents another difference in how we live life. Jean is still unsteady enough on her feet that she will be limited in her ability to get around in bad weather conditions at least for a little while. We had hoped to do a little Christmas shopping today. Jean and Amy cleared out a lot of Jean's clothes yesterday, so I suspect it is getting closer to the transplant night promise/threat Jean made through OR nurse, Pat, that she intends to "shop till she drops." The day is looming closer and closer. So, maybe the weather is on my side! At least for one day.

Later. Well, the weather was not even a minor factor. It cleared in plenty of time for us to get to the Ocean State Job Lot for a little reconnaissance mission, but Jean was not up to full contact shopping just yet. Jean felt all right, not great, just all right and tolerated the walking and movement well. So as long as we watch carefully how much she walks, she will be okay to build her way back up. We picked up some movies for the night, slipped into the Hideaway for an early dinner/late lunch then headed home to watch the movies. A nice quiet, restful evening at home.

12/9/07 DAY 26 AT HOME It's 4:18 AM and I am unable to sleep again tonight. Not certain why, but a few nights like this have happened lately. Even practicing yoga breathing doesn't get me to sleep as it once did. I will have another way to end the day more somnolent so I am not sitting here at the computer looking for things to say. It might be a good time to work on some professional writing I need to catch up on.

I wrote for a couple of hours today before 6:30 AM even rolled around, so it was a productive restless night. Even though tenured, one has to write every so often just to remain relevant and be out there making some noise professionally. I prefer professional presentations to research, but every so often, do get something that either I, or a colleague, want to publish. Jean and I spent another pretty quiet day just doing the necessities. Some wash, a little plumbing work, some exercise (both she and I) and now spending a quiet night "tubing." Ah, the theater of the mindless can be a friend after a long day. That and a rusty nail!

12/10/07 DAY 27 AT HOME Jean had a really positive day today. She felt up to preparing a quick, simple but delicious meal for us both (the only thing she needed help with was the garlic press for which I was conscripted, gladly); folded some wash and did her PT exercises too. I think she is beginning to feel a tad more physically normal, at least I hope so. She received a beautiful, unique gift of a heart from Terri West in Santa Fe that she seemed to immediately embrace along with an inspirational letter of love and support. We need to find the right spot for it. Unfortunately, it came without a return address; so if anyone out there knows Terri's address, please let us know so we can thank her. Or, Terri, since you said in your lovely letter you read this website, maybe you can e-mail me and let me have an address and phone number so Jean can contact you. I think she'd like that. With now less than two weeks left in the semester, I can see the finish line. Only two more late Tuesdays and I am free of the long day schedule that has played some emotional (for me) havoc these past few months. I am also beginning to wonder how much longer we need to keep this website going. Even the kids are asking. So, Jean and I will talk that over and see how she feels about keeping it running or putting it to bed. For today, we will say farewell and thanks again for all your thoughts, cards, letters, gifts and prayers. Jean and I are eternally grateful.

12/11/07 DAY 28 AT HOME The morning started off as usual, but by mid-morning Jean began to get nauseous. Her stomach became upset after eating breakfast, which was not a very heavy breakfast, so we are at a loss as to what happened. Jean got ill just as the PT, Janice, was coming through the door. I don't think this was an emotional response to PT, Jean likes Janice, but obviously this is a mild setback, as I don't see how Jean can get anything out of PT feeling the way she is right now. I am going to stick around longer than usual today just to make sure she feels better before I leave for the university and my late classes.

12/12/07 DAY 29 AT HOME After yesterday's morning fiasco, we took a different tack for breakfast. Apparently something Jean ate upset her stomach so we changed the menu and it looks like she is all right with the changes made. Today will be better if just that nausea stays away. So, we'll see how the day progresses. I have a final exam to administer today; then I will be home early in the afternoon so Jean will not be alone too long.

The day went well. Jean had a very relaxed day. We went out for a light dinner and spent a quiet time visiting friends at the Hideaway. She was able to perform her PT exercises alone today and she seemed to be ambulating pretty well when we went out. So, another day has passed and Jean continues to show progress a little bit at a time.

12/13/07 DAY 30 AT HOME The first 30 days at home have flown by at such a rapid pace that it is hard to remember when Jean was not home. That's a good thing I guess and it speaks to how far she has come already. Progress is measured in time usually, but time, at times, has stood still and at others seemed to have flown by. I think it is really a start and stop kind of progress really. The easiest part of this has been the heart's adjustment to Jean and her to it. That really went medically well right from the onset. It has been the "other stuff" that has taken so much more time -- the med regimens, the changes to them, the daily and twice daily vitals, the PT lessons, getting out and moving around the house. These have taken much longer to effect.

We went to Mohegan Sun for a few hours of fun. Jean held up beautifully, did a lot of walking but held up well. This was her first outing to the casino and I admit I was a bit anxious about her being on the floor of the casino by herself but I know she had to try this to see if she could do it; luckily, she did just fine. So, another milestone has been reached. Progress.

12/14/07 DAY 31 AT HOME We are starting month number two. It has just whizzed right by us. I would have to say that I am surprised at how slow the progress has been in the sense that Jean continues to be so pained and still so weak. But, each day will present a new challenge to gain full strength. That's the task before her. Her heart is fine. All the rest has to come around. If she dedicates herself to the PT workouts and does all the little things she has to get better, she will be just fine.

12/15/07 DAY 32 AT HOME Jean is very tired today. Maybe too much activity yesterday, but Jean seemed to enjoy herself. So, she will rest this morning and maybe later will feel up to a bit of airtime. We'll see how the rest of the day goes. I am concerned that Jean is still in so much pain and has a lot of emotional moments when she simply cries and is overwhelmed by sadness that seems out of kilter with all the good that has come of her transplant. She is unable to explain it to me, as she herself doesn't quite understand the urge to cry. We know that some if it is due to med reactions but we wonder when it might lessen. Jean is not one prone to crying easily and certainly not publicly, yet several times yesterday, she did cry in public for no apparent reason other than being overcome by some emotional urge. On Tuesday, Jean will again go for another biopsy and see the team so at that time she will discuss this with them to get their impressions. Meantime, we keep on doing what we have to keep her going in the right direction toward full recovery and gaining more strength. Her weight has dropped below 120 and that is not what we want. She really needs to go up in weight. How about that for a woman? Wanting to gain weight!

12/16/07 DAY 33 AT HOME A good night's sleep was had by all. The morning greeted us with more snow, mixed with some ice and rain. A fine New England morning it is. Hot coffee and warm jammies kind of morning. Jean had a good night's sleep and awoke felling pretty good. I know she is feeling a bit housebound and has some cabin fever, but today presents a lot of challenges for getting out. We'll see how the weather plays out and maybe we can squeeze in a little field trip. If not, there are movies to see, football to watch (Jean is a big fan! Not.), reading and all sorts of other desultory things to do on a day like this. Mostly, we'll try to stay warm and cozy. I hope that the weather clears away by Tuesday so we don't have any issues getting Jean into New Haven for her next biopsy. Jean had a really good day after all. We were able to get out for a little brunch and picked up some videos for the day. Then, later I got to watch the Giants gag on prime time TV. Can they ever win a home game?

12/17/08 DAY 34 AT HOME This morning I got a YouTube video from my friends in NJ, the Botts, about our favorite hot dog place, Rutt's Hutt. If you have never been there, you don't know what you're missing. The best hot dog anywhere in the world. And even though I gave up eating meat years ago, I will break the fast for a Rutt's dog with onions and home made secret recipe relish. I took Chris there last summer for his maiden voyage when we were on the road to a Yankee game with Bill and John Sloan. He had never been and had the best dog ever. Great way to start the day walking down memory lane with a hot dog in your hand! Jean is still in bed as I write this morning. She remarked last night that she was pretty tired. She and I made some homemade chicken soup yesterday. So, she was on her feet doing some 'therapy' in the kitchen. I see that as a real good sign that she wants to get up and moving around more. The pain gets to her late at night so when we went to bed, she did comment that she was sore. I think this is a good sort of sore because it means she's using her muscles and they are responding to the workload by getting painful as they rebuild. She will be up soon for meds and vitals so we'll see how the night restored her.

Today, Jean received some gifts from friends around the country. One from CO, from long-time friend Browning a Christmas gift; another from our friends, the Schmidts, from MA sent us a tin of homemade cookies. The calories keep a coming! I just wish Jean would eat all this food so I don't have to go to Weight Watchers afraid to get on the scale! Ugh. Jean took it very easy today trying to get her strength up from yesterday's exertion. PT did not come today although we expected her. We had a little excitement today too as we lost power for a couple of hours triggering a little concern about what we might have to do in the event we did not get it back by nightfall. Luckily, it came back about 5:25, so we were spared but I think we'll have to think about what plans we need in the event of this occurrence on a more extended basis. Jean will need to be kept safe in such circumstances; her meds, her machinery and other things she needs to get through a night are portable so we should be okay as long as we can find them. Our crank-style emergency lights came in handy when the sun set.

12/18/07 DAY 35 AT HOME These are the hardest days, these Tuesdays with biopsies. Jean does not look forward to them so she sleeps fitfully the night before, and of course the early morning rising is not her favorite event adding to the angst of these days. Yet, she troops on. The most glaring issue right now seems to be Jean's increasing weight loss. She is down to 115 lbs which is now over 30 lbs lighter than she was when this all began in September. She eats reasonably well compared to how she was eating toward the end of her pre-transplant days when eating made her feel really bad as her heart was struggling to keep her body alive. But now, there is no reason she can't eat and she does eat, but just can't seem to get any weight on her bones. She looks much too frail and I worry that she will be weakened to the point where if she falls she could really hurt herself. So, we hope that today we can get some attention to this problem that will reverse the trend. And, we pray that the good news on heart rejection continues to be good news. She has always had good results, so we anticipate that to continue. More later as the day unfolds. Jean is scheduled for 9:30 AM biopsy, which by hospital time could be anywhere from 9:30 AM to midnight!

10:45 PM I just got home from the university after the final exam for my graduate management class. Jean got through another round of biopsy and blood draws today. She was delayed when a Life Star emergency came in while she was in waiting area. But, despite that she was out about 1:15 and on her way out to lunch with Aimee then home by about 2:30. No lab or biopsy results have been called in to us yet, but by tomorrow, we should have something definitive. Meanwhile, Jean has the after-biopsy pain in her neck where they snake down the probe, so she will get to bed and rest and likely sleep in a little bit tomorrow morning. I'm going to join her in a few minutes.

12/19/07 DAY 36 AT HOME We received good news again today that Jean is not having any rejection based on the latest biopsy results; and, she can reduce the Prednisone and Lasix a bit each day too. A little better each time the meds are reduced, as this is quite a maintenance challenge to say the least. There are about 28 meds a day so any time there is a reduction that helps make things a bit easier all around. Jean continues to feel pain in her back and chest as is to be expected, but I see little signs that she is coming around -- working a little bit in the kitchen, wanting to get out each day, planning things she wants to accomplish, walking and bending a little here and there. Her favorite thing lately is to get in front of the fireplace and warm herself up. I get to blow snow with a new snow blower! Seems about right and fair, huh?

12/20/07 DAY 37 AT HOME PT arrives this morning to begin again working on the various exercises for building Jean's strength. I will be gone most of the day wrapping up the last final exam and posting grades and things like that so; I will not be around till this afternoon. So, if you are willing, today might be a good day to give Jean a call after noon. The holiday mail has been done, a short mailing list this year since Jean was physically not up to her usual level of excitement about Christmas. Generally, we are traveling to CO for the holidays with our hearts in our throats worrying about how the altitude might affect Jean's heart while we're there. That is another problem we can scratch off out list of worries this year and perhaps forever. That would be nice. We always said we wanted to travel when the kids grew up and we were free to go, now maybe we can actually plan to one day soon go where we have always wanted to go -- places like Italy, Greece, UK, France, etc. Would be nice.

Susan von Reichenbach visited Jean today bearing some homemade soup to keep us hearty. Jean needs that a lot more than I do, that's for sure. Tonight we will enjoy a brief celebration of semester's end with dinner out and some adult beverages for me. I earned them!

12/21/07 DAY 38 AT HOME It must be getting close to Christmas, as Jean has become recipe consultant for family and friends, fielding calls from all over the nation on how to do this and that. She may not be banging those pots and pans, but she can still consult with the best of them. For this year at least, Pasta Vita will be supplying the Christmas dinner for the Panza family and yours truly will be doing the re-heating. Someone has to do the dirty work! After all the years Jean has made Christmas dinner for the hordes of children, grandchildren, friends and lovers, this year will be her year to take the day off. And, if I want to eat, I better do this.

Late this evening, Chris and Alia sprang their surprise Christmas on us. We were both very touched by their generosity and pleased with the thoughtfulness of their gifts. Jean got a new TV, flat panel with closed-captioning that she needs increasingly nowadays and I got a 35 mm Canon camera to play with. All I wanted for Christmas I got November 1st, but this was nice too. In the mail, I also received a gift from my other children (Joe, Stacie and Amy), new special sunglasses to protect my eyes when I am out playing softball in the spring and summer. They have special *lenses for maximum eye protection from harmful rays and glare. Very chic and very practical as well. Beats the heck out of a sweater I will never use! These will get lots of use. They were not gift wrapped so when I opened the box, I knew what my gift was. I am not into surprises like some folks are. Besides, I had hinted very strongly that I wanted these so that the kids would not waste time guessing what dear old dad wanted for Christmas. I am easy to please. Easy, but not cheap!*

12/22/07 DAY 39 AT HOME Jean is very excited that her weight has held from yesterday. So am I. I went to Weight Watchers this morning after missing a fair number of weeks since Jean came home and, lo and behold, I am up only 1 lb! That was pretty good considering that it has been so long since I have attended a meeting and weighed in. I try to stay true to the plan and, by gum, it worked. So, now that I am off from work for a while, I can get back on the program in earnest and see if I can't chip off that 1lb and then some to get to my target weight. I've been trying to get back to my original weight, 7 lbs 13 oz, for most of my life! But I will settle for 195. Not quite there yet, but closing in. I got to use the new TV tonight with the built-in DVD player. Pretty slick. We were trying to figure out how old the old TV was and, best I can remember, we bought that TV when Stacie was still in grade school. She has now been married for 12 years and has two children so I think that TV served us pretty well. Still works fine but just doesn't have the closed-captioning feature we did not need then but do now. Our generation gave up its hearing so that the world could enjoy rock n' roll music like we did. I hope this generation appreciates our contribution to the "advancement" of civilization for which we paid so dearly in the diminution or loss of our hearing! It's amazing how many of our conversations are interspersed with the endless question, "what?" My father was a drummer in his youth and then spent many years in hostile work environments where noise was prominent adding insult to injury. Jean's mom was hard of hearing and her sister is also, so both sides of our families have marked hearing impairments. My mom, now 93, has hearing aids but at 93 still hears remarkably well when she wants to! Whoever dubbed these the "Golden Years" must have been a marketing guy! Golden? Maybe he misspelled it and meant it to say "Olden." But, as I always say, any day above the grass, is a good day.

12/23/07 DAY 40 AT HOME Quite a bit of shopping activity today. A trip to New Haven to pick up meds at Yale, then IKEA, that was a real workout but not nearly as busy I would have thought 2 days before Christmas. Then, lunch at Chili's in East Haven, then Job Lot in Old Saybrook. Jean put in a full day of walking and held up really well. That's a good sign. I, on the other hand, got home and had to assemble the purchase from IKEA that took the entire second half of the Giant game so I missed much of that, but another job was well done by Panza's Home Improvements and Nursing Inc. Jean did not participate in this fiasco but was cheering from another room -- cheering me, not the Giants! Big help, there. We got a phone call from our friends, the Schmidts (of Christmas cookie gift fame) and the Sloans, wishing us Merry Christmas. The Sloans are planning a trip to see us in January to which we look forward. We received a nice e-mail from our friends in Memphis, Mouse and Cissy Brown, sending their well wishes to Jean. We haven't seen them for many years but consider them dear friends from our years in the South. We spent some holidays with them when we lived there. They were always kind, welcoming and gracious hosts even taking us to MS to their summer cottage for a long weekend.

12/24/07 DAY 41 AT HOME Jean reported this morning that she has gained another pound. Another good sign. She is beginning to look more fit and getting back some of her stamina. She reported this morning that the pain is subsiding a little bit and is now unendurable without relief early morning and late at night, but during the day she is feeling all right. She has pretty much stopped using the Vicodin except for half a tablet once in a while at night, instead using just Tylenol. The fact that after all she did yesterday that she felt good this morning is significant. Before, if she had expended a lot of effort one day, the next she would need to rest a lot. But today she was up before I was, was making the bed this morning (!) while I was puttering around cleaning up and moving furniture made unnecessary by yesterday's purchase and by the new TV. I schlepped an ottoman and the old TV to the basement and picked up the disposed carton and stuff I put on the deck while assembly was underway. I found IKEA's pictorial-only instructions a bit tedious and hard to follow since they use no words to assist the selection of pieces and parts to avoid language translations for their many ports of call. But, a little verbal help would have been good. Luckily, it was a pretty simple storage unit so I was able to figure it out but anything even a bit more complex would have been a challenge without words! Today, Jean wants to, guess what? Do some shopping! Then, we are invited to a party of "regulars" at the Hideaway, later on, at which we will make an appearance for certain, as they were the very first to send Jean a bouquet when she first went into the hospital and since we are regulars. There were many nights I ended my day eating there after leaving Jean at Yale so they were privy to much of her progress, or lack thereof, during the time when great uncertainty was abounding. Great folks, patrons, staff, bartenders and owners alike. It should be fun and will be our only Christmas party this year, but next year!

12/25/07 DAY 42 AT HOME Merry Christmas.

We are thrilled to be able to celebrate this Christmas with the hope of new life and improved health for Jean as we face the coming months when she will resume more normal activity, will have more stamina and be able to be pain free. It goes without saying that all of you, who have faithfully prayed and let Jean and me know your thoughts and prayers have been with her and with me, have made this Christmas one of the most special of all. We have enjoyed many Christmases together, 42 to be exact, many of those with our children, and more recently with our grandchildren too, so we know what Christmas means to us, but this one, this one is really different in a way that is hard to describe. Jean's is the most unusual Christmas gift one can imagine. That a family we do not know yet and have yet to meet, could give of their child's body to make Jean's whole again is a gift beyond imagining. As they celebrate their first Christmas without their son, and I hesitate to use the word celebrate, perhaps mark is better, without him, I can barely imagine what their own hearts must feel like this morning -- heavy, leaden, sorrowful and pained come to my mind -- but I hope that maybe one day when they get to meet Jean and learn of this website, they will come to know what their gift has meant to her and to all of us. In the season when gift giving has become synonymous with commercial, material gifts, I am reminded that those gifts will one day break, wear out, go out of style, be useless in some way or another, but the gift of life endures for many years beyond the immediate gratification of opening a box wrapped in paper. This gift was wrapped in pain, terror, loss and yet hope was delivered and received. Quite a gift I'd say. We do not as yet know the circumstances of the donor's demise, nor do we even know his name or the family's whereabouts, but one day soon we hope to put those questions to rest and be able to thank them face to face as befits this wondrous deed of generosity in the midst of an awful, terrible time in their lives. We pray for them, as the holidays must be a dreadfully painful time as this is all still so raw for them I imagine. I hope that they intuitively know how much we thank them until we get to do it for real in person. I will always remember Jean's first utterance upon coming out of her induced coma state when we told her the heart came from a 21 year-old man, she wept quietly still unable to speak, her voice still affected by the insertion of tube in her throat, when she heard she mouthed the words, "That poor mother." Today, we pray that that poor mother knows we send our undying love, gratitude and appreciation for all that she and her family sacrificed that day on our behalf and on behalf of however many others they helped that November 1st, 2007. May God bless them today and every day, easing their loss and salving their anguish. Today, I wish them a Christmas filled with peace if not merriment. Thank you.

Chris and Alia left late this afternoon traveling to AZ by car. They left earlier than expected as they were watching a storm system coming through where they have to travel and thought if they got started earlier they might be able to navigate around it or beat it as it travels eastward. At any rate, we were saddened by their departure, as they have been a big part of the day-to-day events here this past year and a few months. We, of course, wish them nothing but the best as they return home to their friends and her family with a fresh start that we hope will propel them on their way to peace and happiness in the desert of AZ. But, for both of us, there is a certain emptiness already as we grapple with the idea of once again being empty nesters. We did that once before and found out we were pretty good at it, but that was long before the heart disease that eventually hit Jean. We will see how we do this time around. I will of course miss Chris' strength, as he was so important to me the days leading up and the day of Jean's transplant. They had delayed their leaving back then to be a part of the events and to lend support when the time came. Now, we send them on their way to what we pray will be their destinies for a happy life together until we see them again. I asked Chris to consider meeting us in CO next Christmas so we all have something to shoot for and to give Jean a target of being all healed and ready to travel this time next year. Chris, in his own unique and deeply felt way, left notes for each of us so that we would be comforted. He was able to communicate his feelings and thoughts to us quite well. We are proud of how well he has done since coming to CT to get his health back. I will especially miss him during baseball season, as we were able to watch the Yankees every night and enjoy the company as father and son and as grown men who are friends as well. Ah, well that's why we raise them, so they can leave us and spread their own wings. So, Christmas catches us by surprise in a way we could not expect. Now, it is just the two of us!

12/26/07 DAY 43 AT HOME Good signs abound. Jean was up early this morning, straightening things up! That means she is getting ticked off about conditions around the house, giving me orders on the honey dos and in essence taking charge of her home. Now, with Chris and Alia safely on their way, they made it to OH last night, she is reclaiming the place and deciding how she wants things. I will be on call I'm sure for all menial tasks that need doing and have already assigned myself the task of painting the main bathroom to spruce it up, which needed doing but now can be done as it will be off line without the kids using it every day. John, Barbara, niece Allison and nephew Kevin will be here later today so Jean will have some company other than me for a change of pace that'll do her good. Now, I'm off to run errands and do some food shopping, yippee!

12/27/07 DAY 44 AT HOME Jean had a restless night last night. She seemed to be unable to get herself settled and complained about her legs twitching. I wonder if she isn't having some muscle spasms related to either medications or perhaps to her muscles repairing since she is moving around so much more actively now. I think she still tends to see everything in the context of heart disease, which would be expected, but maybe this is one of those things that just isn't at all related but is being attributed to that errantly. PT is scheduled today at some point in the morning, so we can ask about that. Today, we had our pictures taken for renewal of our expiring passports. Although we haven't needed them recently for any travel out of the country, we thought it best to renew them so when we are clear to travel again, we may choose to go where we had always talked about going when we were older and free of the demands of children, etc. We made a little excursion to Wal-Mart, too. Jean wanted to look at new comforters so we went to the Home Goods after that and picked up something we liked, but then when we got home, she saw something she liked better in a catalog that had arrived that day and so we ordered another by nightfall. Now, we will have more comforters from which to choose! PT never did show up so we are not sure what happened to that appointment.

12/28/07 DAY 45 AT HOME Yesterday seems emblematic of life on the other side of transplant. Things are beginning to become more normalized again. Although Jean still tires pretty easily, I see her performing more independent tasks, moving around more and even complaining about how much she sits around doing "nothing." In her case, cabin fever is a good sign. If she is wanting to get around more that tells me she is feeling more like her old self. I'll be happy to accommodate her any time she wants to get out as I see her getting more stamina, improved strength, she hasn't fallen in weeks now, and generally just being more active. She still can't negotiate stairs too easily, but entering and leaving the house are easier for certain. She is better. Today, we'll see how she feels after the activity yesterday. PT did arrive today and worked with Jean and then released her from further PT services, so she is done with that aspect and is now on her own until cardiac rehab kicks in. That will be ordered by the doctors following an upcoming visit.

12/29/07 DAY 46 AT HOME Jean had planned to get out this morning to look for a new coat but after morning meds and showering, she felt too much pain to move about, so we postponed our plans for now waiting to see if the pain subsides and she improves enough to get out for a little walking around. Guess I will go back to my to do list and wait for the football games to start around 1 PM with UConn playing in the Meineke Car Care and Muffler Hole Bowl, or whatever the silly thing is called. Corporate sponsorship has now made it possible for 64 college teams to go bowling, even a couple with 6 - 6 records. Whatever happened to pride? Tonight, the Giants will get a shot at breaking New England's fans' hearts like they did a few years back when my Broncos came into Giants Stadium 13 - 0 only to be stopped by the Giant defense. Patriots' fans should note that that year the Broncos lost that game, finished 13 - 3 but went on to win the Super Bowl. It'd be better for the Patriots to lose this week than any of the next 3 weeks when one loss finishes your season. Should be good especially if the weather is awful and Giants can run the ball the way they did last week against the Bills. We'll see how it goes. Meanwhile, my Broncos are just playing out the string to go home for the off-season. Won't be long for pitchers and catchers to report to spring training. C'mon spring training!

Eve Todd came by to have some tea and dessert with Jean after which we went out for short shopping trip to buy Jean a new coat and some slacks. She seems to be rebounding *again. I was also able to return our master bath to its normal operating condition now that Jean no longer needs assistance there. Another good sign that she is strengthening a little bit more each day. With the painting I did yesterday in the main bath, we now have both bathrooms back to full service as we gradually restore our home to its previous condition. The nest is empty again so we have free access to every room in the house. Next renovation is the study. Gotta do something with this room so it is more serviceable as an office. Chris and Alia are safely in Phoenix having made the trip in only 3 days' time without any weather problems. They left Christmas day and arrived in AZ on the 28th. So, their new chapter begins, as does our next chapter.*

12/30/07 DAY 47 AT HOME I noticed this morning, as I was updating the site that tomorrow marks the 60th day since Jean's transplant. It has gone by so quickly and, happily, so smoothly that we have hardly noticed the passage of the time even though I have been chronicling it all these days. Maybe that's the point of all this -- to slow it down, digest it, mark it and move ahead. In the next stage, if there is such a thing, we will see Jean's return to her former self, maybe mixed in with her new self, as she starts to grapple with the realities of having another human being's heart beating in her chest. Up to now, we have not spoken much about the effects of that knowledge, but I suspect that once Jean gets into the support group network the existential elements of this experience will begin to press on her mind and emotions. Up till now, she has had to concentrate on learning to walk, move, take her meds properly and the physical maintenance routines. Yet, there is the 800 lb gorilla in the room waiting to be noticed. I think this next phase will be quite a ride for us both. It is at this next point we may get to connect with the donor family, too.

12/31/07 DAY 48 AT HOME For some inexplicable reason, Jean was unable to sleep last night. She finally gave up the idea and got up to retreat to the family room where she would be able to watch TV and so as not to disturb me. This morning when I awoke she was already awake telling me she was up till about 3 AM, so she could not have gotten more than a few hours of sleep since I was up before 7:30. This is another issue that we need to watch carefully; sleep deprivation is certainly not a good thing. We have reservations at a very nice restaurant in Waterford, called Filomena's, for tonight, so I hope Jean will get some rest during the day and be able to enjoy our celebratory dinner. I noted today is the 60th day post transplant—two months have gone by already, just like that. New Year's day will begin the third month of Jean's recovery. And, just as I thought yesterday was a turning point, one which augured well for Jean's return to normalcy, where she was walking around, wanting to get out to the casino, etc., the night presented a set of new questions. We both thought that with all the activity Jean had at Mohegan, she would be exhausted and get a really good night's sleep. But, alas, not the way it worked at all! I can't wait for those days that we can count on as average, normal, routine days. I wonder if there will be any again.

In the afternoon, we went to Home Depot to dink around and get some ideas for a cabinet I want to build in the family room but to no avail as Home Depot is only a semi-custom cabinet making retailer rather than a custom cabinet making retailer as I came to find out from talking to the cabinet expert there, a guy named Bob. Interestingly, he mentioned that he could himself make what I am looking for, but is prohibited from doing so as an employee because of conflict of interest! Imagine, working for Home Depot one has to relinquish the right to make extra income to collect a near minimum wage salary! And, he could not tell me who he knew who might be able to do what I needed done.

What a great country we have become, huh? I suggest a new slogan for Home Depot, "You can do it, but we can't do it for you or with you." We also looked at some refrigerators for ideas on replacing ours next summer. Of course, its being a men's toy store. I couldn't leave without something. So, I picked up some metal storage shelves to add shelf space to the basement where we can store more stuff. It is here where the line blurs, as my storage space becomes Jean's need to store stuff on my shelves! And, my partner in shopping saw a lamp she really liked for the family room, so we picked that up as well.

After a lot of walking through Home Depot, we went to lunch at Olive Garden, had some soup and salad and then went home. We were out for a couple of hours so I knew Jean was tiring. When we got home I assembled the shelves and the lamp while she napped. When she awoke, I had a sense that Jean was still pretty tired. After a brief discussion she agreed with my sense that she really was not up to going out for a late dinner, our reservation being for 8 PM. So, we canceled our reservation choosing not to go out for dinner. So instead we spent just an hour visiting friends at the Hideaway, were home by 7:30, watched some TV and went to bed early. For the first time I can remember we were not awake to see the New Year ring in at Times Square. Either we are getting to that magical age where one begins to care less about such events, or we were just plain old tired. I'm going with tired for now with the reservation that I might come back to the other reason if the facts support it.

2008 Begins The NEW Year in more ways than one

1/1/08 DAY 49 AT HOME I awoke to a frigid cold in the house. The furnace apparently shut itself down during the night. I hastily dressed and ran to the basement to check out the boiler, its Cyclops' red eye blinking at me reporting that it was indeed off! I pressed the red reset button and it jumped on eager to do its job of heating the house. Jean is still in bed so I hope to have the house back up to normal room temperature by the time she arises. Right now it is 58 degrees in here and I am trying to keep my fingers moving so they can type, inadequately at best, for I am the master of the old hunt and peck technique. We have a propane fireplace we can use if this doesn't keep us warm, so there is a back up plan. I sure hope this is not an augury of the year to come! My sister and our friend Susan have invited us to their homes for daytime open houses so we very likely will be spending some time out of the house today visiting with some family -- nieces and nephews -- neighbors, and friends. It should be nice so I hope Jean feels up to it. We'll know when she gets up how the day might play out. The house is just now beginning to warm slightly so I hope that Jean stays in bed a little longer until the house warms up more. I don't want her exposed to this extreme cold. There seems to me nothing colder than a house that has no heat. I always noticed that feeling when looking at homes when we were house shopping. Cold homes feel colder than the outdoors it seems. Well, I am off to make some coffee. Today, it will feel extra warm!

We went to one of our invited open houses, the one at my sister's home, and Jean had a very relaxed afternoon, staying for a few hours and getting a chance to reunite with my niece, grand nieces, grand nephew, nephews-in-law, the newest addition, another girl, et al. So, the day was nice and full. However, when it came time for bed, Jean found herself unable to get to sleep easily even after using medication to assist her. She became emotional again about some swelling she thinks is contributing to her steady, but now unusual, weight gain -- a pound or more a day. I comforted her as best I could but I know that that is not enough to allay her fears, which are a carryover from her previous CHF days. She continues to see symptoms through that experience.

1/2/08 DAY 50 AT HOME Jean awoke before I did this morning, but I heard her rumbling about so I got up to check if she was okay. She had already weighed herself and her weight was up again although the swelling she had observed the previous evening was down. Nonetheless, the VNA nurse called after Jean transmitted her daily vitals over the phone system to ask about the weight gain making it a concern enough that she, the nurse, was going to phone the doctor. Jean called the nurse from the transplant team, Joan, to see what if anything she needed to do, but Joan was unable to give her any direct advice, choosing to check with the doctor first and then saying she would call back. Needless to say, this is a harrowing development if edema again presents itself. It can be an ongoing problem and one we had hoped would be rectified with a new heart. So, we wait to hear.

1/3/08 DAY 51 AT HOME The night was better last night. Jean was again first to arise, as we have a pretty full day ahead of us. I have a chiropractic appointment this morning to which Jean will come as we then drive from West Haven right over to Yale for a midday luncheon support group meeting with the post transplant survivors and their families. It will be Jean's first one, my second, so I expect it might be pretty emotional for her, as she will for the first time see and hear other's tell their stories and she too might be telling hers. Afterwards, Jean will be visiting her doctor at the transplant team offices to see if they can determine why she is gaining weight so fast. They want to rule out any serious issues such as swelling although I don't see any. It is possible that edema is gathering somewhere other than her extremities, such as her abdomen, and they can check for that while she is New Haven. I hope that this will put the matter to rest, as she worries so much about this. They moved this appointment up from next week to get a handle on this before it gets any worse. So, some cause for concern that we hope to get remedied today. By late afternoon, we should know what is going on. Then, Browning Tinker, our friend from CO will be arriving and that means Jean will have some company other than me, which is good for her.

Good news all around. Jean enjoyed the support group asking questions and meeting fellow survivor Christine. The extremely cold weather kept the crowd small, but Joan, the transplant team nurse, went over in great detail a rather thorough and information-filled handout on post-transplantation. Afterwards, we went to Jean's appointment with the team doctors and there, Jean had an echocardiogram, and other tests all of which came back just fine. So, her swelling is really nothing to be concerned about; her weight gain is the same. A change of meds was made to switch one of her immunosuppression meds from Neoral to Prograf, intended to reduce some of the problems with lanugo (downy soft hair growth). All in all, Jean is thriving and doing as well as she can do. She needed to hear that, and frankly, so did I! Browning arrived this afternoon and was waiting for us when we got home. So, I think I will watch football, again! There isn't any baseball right now, so football will have to suffice. In the mail today, we received two lovely figurines from Stacie's lifelong friend, Allison, and her husband Joe, a woman and a man with hearts of gold! This gift was filled with symbolism and touching to say the least. Oh, and the new bedspread came in too, so I will be installing (?) that tomorrow when the painter is finished with the bedroom. At least this won't require any tools.

We went for dinner and had a nice time. Jean and Browning got caught up on things, as she had not seen Jean since before she was hospitalized. I heard them laughing a lot so I know they were glad to be sharing the good times. As for me, I was engaged in ticking off the patrons next to me and Jim, my old softball teammate (and aspiring novelist and son of a former CT state legislator) and now barkeep at the Hideaway, about the Iowa caucuses answering their questions about who I would vote for, which was great fun. They were very interested in trying to affix a label to my politics, never an easy or simple thing and one I try purposely to be vague about because I mistrust the labeling of people by what their politics say about them. I believe that we are a complicated mix of liberal, conservative, libertarian, socialist, communist and any other "ist" depending on the ox we want to gore (not Al) or the issue that has us ticked off that particular day. At least, I think we ought to be a mix with an open mind so that we do not fall into the trap of mindlessly voting for a party! That is just too easy and a bit lazy if you ask me. Anyway, I had some fun with them, although I'd venture to say that they probably would characterize their experience as something other than fun when summing me up. Jim and I finished our conversation when they left. His insights were a hoot, as he regaled me with stories about how his dad, a staunch Republican, could defend his decision to vote for Bush a second time when he knew all the objective facts and reasons why he should not have were right before his eyes. In a nutshell, even though this is a man who is well-educated, an attorney, knows politics really well having spent much of his life in them, concluded, "because I am a Republican," as his reason for voting for Bush. See, there it is, party over reason! Makes me frightened for the future in this next election and for any national election if a person as bright as Jim's dad, will fall back on that as the reason he voted for a candidate. Imagine what the many uninformed might do. Oh, they'd do the same thing! Or worse, they wouldn't vote at all.

1/4/08 DAY 52 AT HOME Today will be a girls' day. With Browning here, Jean will be preoccupied and busy doing whatever these two miscreants can cook up. I would be pretty safe in assuming that shopping, in some form, will be included. Browning belongs to the same athletic club Jean does, the one that considers shopping an athletic event or sport. As for me, I will be doing something else, gladly. Jean had her last VNS visit today, so she is now on her own without PT or RN services meaning that she is turning the corner and headed on the fast track to full recovery. Next week, she will have her next biopsy after two weeks without one. The spacing will continue, as she proves more resistant to rejection. We hope and pray for that.

1/5/08 DAY 53 AT HOME Saturday comes a-calling. I wonder what this day will bring. I am leaving for Weight Watchers in about 2 minutes so will have to get back to update.

The Website Shuts Down

Daily Update: 1/5/08 Jean has asked me to shut down the website with the intent that all of you who have been faithful readers keep her in your prayers through the next 9 months. By then, Jean will be a year past transplant and her status will be well-known and hopefully she will be well on her way to full recovery in whatever form that takes. Please feel free to call, visit, write or otherwise communicate any time you wish. Jean is open to everyone and is feeling more like her old self than ever. So, on her behalf and mine as well, we want to thank you for being with us throughout this time of great challenge and peril. With all of you rooting and praying, she and I have been able to endure what we never could fully understand without having gone through it. Like we always have, we went through it together, holding hands, loving each other fully and unconditionally, but fully aware that at any moment what we had so prized, our relationship and our marriage, were in harm's way. But even knowing the danger, we felt blessed that we had each other, our children, our families and friends to sustain us. And, we always knew that God would be the final arbiter of our fate. We know now, this was not the time He chose. Instead, He sent us a reminder that we are all interdependent and that one's love for another, even a stranger, is the manifestation of His love and what He wishes for us to do in our lives—give so that others may benefit even from our loss and pain. We await the time we can meet the donor's family, as that will be the culmination of this life-altering experience and we hope in some small way we can reciprocate, although our gift to them would pale compared to theirs to us, by thanking them personally for what they have done for my beloved Jean.

Chapter 4 - 2008 and Beyond

Beginning of the End or the End of a Beginning

Our second Thanksgiving day since Jean's transplant is about to arrive and we continued to be thrilled at how much we have to be thankful for this year as last. Since last year, we have added a second birthday to Jean's year. We went out for a beautiful dinner at Tuscany on November 1st. Joining us were Amy, Terese, John & Barbara, Cookie and Frank. We ate in the library room and were treated to tableside serenading, and a wonderful gesture of support from Jim Wilkinson, VP of Player Development, whom I had met earlier and who had marveled at our celebration and wanted to contribute in some way. He came by, arranged for us to receive a wonderful gift allowance toward dinner and toasted Jean's successful year. Later this month, we will travel to NJ for Thanksgiving with Barbara and John, Uncle Lou and Aunt Rita, then we'll visit with my buddies and their wives on Saturday with another celebration of Jean at the Park Tavern where we hung out as high school knuckleheads and young married couples. Billy & Pat, Denny & Cindy and Brian & Carol will be there to join in.

Only Billy & Pat have seen Jean since all this happened so the others will be amazed at what they see when they see Jean. Can't wait for that; oh, and my birthday will be the day before that so I will celebrate another click off the clock with the guys I bled with and grew into a man with! It'll be a day for reminiscing and old jokes, but there's nothing better than old friends to make you feel warm and to remind you where you started.

Chapter 5 - Starting to Make Contact — The First Communication

The last 12 months have flown by. Jean continues to make progress and is now safely past any possible problems other than rejection, which is no small thing, and which will be a lifelong challenge. Meantime, she has finished cardiac rehab, worked her way back to reasonably healthy condition, maintained an ideal weight and is back to wearing size 6 or 8 clothes. She has regained her confidence. Jean has begun to drive, and has even driven some highway, which she was unable to do before.

But more significantly, we have made contact with the donor family through correspondence provided by New England Organ Bank. We heard not a word until now, so we are excited that this may be the time when we get to meet Jean's donor's family and find out how this mystical event came to pass. Life will be different from this point on, of that I am certain. We are entering a place we have never been before after all that Jean has endured, I am left to wonder if this next phase will be what we hope it can be. Only time will tell.

Chapter 6 - The Next Phase

For many valid medical and psychological reasons, contact between donors and recipients is handled and managed by the organ donation organizations. In this way, correspondence is anonymous until both families communicate their desire to meet. The organ donation organization then arranges via mail the first contact, which in our case, and we assume in all cases, is through written communication so that the next step, meeting one another, can be arranged by the parties involved and then the organ donation folks back away and let whatever happens happen. It is done this way so that identities can be protected, privacy can be assured, and people can decide on their own whether or not each wishes to be in contact with the other.

Jean and I always believed that we wanted to know as much as we could about her donor. Right from the outset, we believed that the only sincere way to thank those involved would be face to face. Yet, at the same time, we knew we had no control over the other family's desire to meet us or not. But having heard the various stories at the support group meetings, we knew that some people never hear from the donor family, others do, but not right away and that there is no such thing as typical or average when it comes to this aspect of transplantation. Besides, we knew that Jean's first concern after she was informed about her donor was to utter the words, "Oh, that poor mother." I knew she would never be at peace with this if she could not reach her hand out and touch this other mother. Jean's heart has always been large in the metaphorical sense. Having a new heart to live with did not change her disposition to still be loving, reaching and building relationships. The big heart metaphor was unchanged despite which heart she had beating inside her. So, we hoped that we could establish contact and our wishes were reciprocated, as you will soon see.

The following is the letter Jean sent to the organ donation organization to hold if the donor family ever contacted them with an interest in communicating with her. At that time, we had no way of knowing that it would ever be read by them or would ever be responded to by them. We relied on the hope that had gotten us this far; knowing that a family that could make such a sacrifice and such a hard decision would be interested in knowing how this all turned out and could somehow answer the question, "was this the right thing to do?" "Was it worth it?"

March 15, 2008

Dear Donor Family,

Please forgive the impersonal salutation above but I am unaware of your name at this time. Nonetheless, I write to tell you how you have come to be a part of my life forever.

On November 1st, 2007, in the midst of what, I can only surmise, was your worst day, you made the decision to grant me the gift of a new heart. That day, I went from a person with a fading heart from congestive heart failure to a person with a future I had long ago abandoned. I had made preparations with my family and fully expected that I would never leave the hospital. Yet, that fateful day, you allowed me the opportunity to once again make plans to spend time with my husband, my children, my grandchildren, family and friends. For your wonderful loving gesture of faith, I want to say, inadequately in words, thank you. You are blessed each night as I offer my prayers of thanks to a God who saw fit to bring us together in a plan much larger than either of us could have envisioned.

On behalf of all my loved ones and from the depths of my heart, your heart gift to me, I wish to thank you and want you to know I will forever cherish this heart, you and your family member for the greatest imaginable gift one human being can give another. May your loss be lessened by the knowledge that what you gave to me has brought great joy to many, who, though once strangers, are now inextricably bound together for all time. As my family and I this week begin our celebration of Easter, as is our custom, we are vividly and personally reminded that all life involves death and resurrection, time and time again. I am grateful that my 'resurrection' became possible through the wonderful strength and courage of strangers. I hope that that knowledge somehow lightens your loss knowing that my rebirth is so much more than symbolic. And yet, we, my family and I, too mourn and grieve with you knowing how hard this must have been for you.

If ever you wish to connect with me, I would consider it a privilege to meet you and to bring your family into my family as you have done for me with your kindness and spirit. Then, we need never be strangers again.

Thank you. And may God bless you in so many ways for your spirit of love and giving. I am eternally grateful to you.

Sincerely,

Jean (Last names and return addresses could not be used at the writing of this letter by instruction of the organ donation organization pending a return interest.)

November 2008

Eight months since Jean's letter was mailed had flown by without a word until we received a letter from the New England Organ Bank dated October 31st, 2008, telling us that the mother of Jean's donor accepted Jean's letter in August 2008, then called the NEOB to inquire about making direct contact. Enclosed with the letter were forms for Jean to sign, a general release and a recipient consent, which, if signed, would waive the right of confidentiality and allow the facilitation of direct contact between the families. We were thrilled to get this. Another one of our hopes was realized and we were getting close to the day when we could actually say thank you *in person*.

We knew that this day, if it ever came, would be a very emotional event for us and surmised it would be the same for them. But our excitement began to grow.

Our First Contact

Direct contact from the donor's family was first made when we received a note card from Paula Flint of Amesbury MA, dated November 12, 2008. In it she wrote that not a day goes by that she does not think of Jean and our family. She knew Jean's first name from the original letter we sent NEOB last year and now of course had our last name and home address. She urged Jean to keep writing. We were thrilled, excited and so joyful that we were a step closer to putting a face to a name. This set off in us a series of question all over again. We assumed that Paula was the mother of the donor, but what if she was his wife? Trying to judge the handwriting, as if we were sleuths, we concluded that it was youthful so maybe she was a young widow. This not knowing was driving us a little crazy. But, we sensed that things were moving along and soon we would get to meet.

We now knew the name of the donor's mother, Paula, where she lived; Amesbury MA, and had received a lovely note card from her telling us that she thinks of Jean every day. Soon, Jean would be addressing a second letter directly to Paula in hopes that we might one day meet face to face and be able to thank her in person for what she made possible with her great courage and act of generosity. Hopefully, this would occur soon. Amesbury is just a few hundred miles from here, about two and half hours away, just north of Boston, so within a short drive. Now, we looked forward to establishing a lasting relationship with Paula and her children.

In Jean's note back to Paula she asked some questions, gave Paula our home phone number so we could now see if she would be willing to get together.

On December 12, 2008, we were contacted by Paula, again. She had let us know that she was the **mother** of Jean's donor. She sent a lovely Christmas card and a Willow Tree figurine of a young man and a heart. Her **son** was Jean's donor. (Jean's first words spoken to Amy and me right after awakening from the transplant and hearing the news that her donor was a 21 year-old man were, "Oh that poor mother." Those words were prophetic even though it took till this day to be sure.) Now we knew and

I knew that Jean would get emotional at the knowledge of this.

The card was signed: Paula, Hayley and Jared. They are the family that so bravely gave their gift to Jean without knowing her. We were beginning to learn a bit more now. Soon, we hoped to meet Paula, Hayley and Jared and be able to thank them face-to-face. Perhaps we could arrange this very shortly after we returned from Denver where we were scheduled to celebrate the Christmas holidays with our children and grandchildren and to see how Jean now handled the altitude with her new heart. It was a really important test for us, because if Jean could handle the altitude, we might then be able to plan our retirement back home so we can be with our children and grandchildren when I am done teaching in a few years. But, we both knew that these holidays were fast approaching but on the other side of them we would have a date with the donor family if we could set that up. What a gift that would be for us!

Sensing that I might be able learn more about Jean's donor and his family, I began a Google search and, lo and behold, I found a news item about a 21 year-old man who died in that area on October 30, 2007, *two days before Jean got her heart*. His name was Drew. We had what I assumed and concluded was the definitive information. He was Drew. He had a mother named Paula, a brother named Jared and a sister named Hayley. That was too much matching information for this to be just coincidence. I could not believe I was fortunate enough to ferret out this information. My imagination was piqued. A line in the piece read, "Although Drew did not communicate verbally, he touched so many lives!" I immediately began to speculate about what that meant and I came to a rushed conclusion that was based on a long career working with children with disabilities that Drew indeed could fit the description of one of those children that I served in my professional life for 27 years! Was that possible? Could it be that God had brought Jean and me full circle, could it be that Drew, my beloved Jean's donor, was a child with cerebral palsy and developmental disabilities? What symmetry that would be! How the advocate in me relished that thought. There had been so many children like this who had been devalued for so many years. I fought against that devaluing and now taught the very principles of valuing such people that this was almost too much to believe. I would have to wait and see when we met Paula if what I suspected was indeed true. I couldn't wait. I was even more excited to meet her after learning all this and felt assured that what I had found was the real thing. Jean was too, as we awaited the next contact and anticipated the very thing we have wanted to do—meet Paula.

Chapter 7 - Prelude to The Meeting

We were now just a short time away from being blessed with the opportunity to meet Jean's donor's mother. Through the coordinated efforts of UNOS and its New England affiliate, we had corresponded with Paula and finally had arranged to meet her face-to-face Sunday, February 8th 2009. Paula wrote to us to tell us of her plans to come to Connecticut for a little rest and relaxation at Foxwoods Casino, just 30 minutes from our home. We agreed to meet her, exchanged cell phone numbers and began the countdown to the time and place, trying to picture what she looked like, what she would say, how she would react, how Jean and I would embrace her, or if she were too uncomfortable for an embrace, what we should do? We had never of course been in this situation. What's the proper way to meet a donor's mother? Who knew? We decided we would just be ourselves and meet her the way we meet anyone—with open arms, open minds and open hearts.

All that week, we were pretty excited but also tentative because we knew how hard this would be. Jean is a quietly emotional person, who does not like to show her emotions on her sleeve. I am more effusive, but this was Jean's moment, not mine. I wanted to be there just to support her if she needed me. Paula agreed to let Jean bring me along since she was bringing a friend, Ron, with her, I suspected for support, too. It would be a powerfully emotional and poignant moment for all of us.

Sunday, February 8th 2009

We scheduled to meet around 12:30 PM at Foxwoods Casino in the Rainmaker Casino, near the Atrium cafe. That morning, to be absolutely certain that we had everything correctly understood, I called Paula's cell phone, to ask how we might identify her. She told me she would be wearing a brown sweater, brown boots and had blond hair. We set out around 11:30 to make sure we got there in plenty of time, since we had not been to Foxwoods in years. I was not at all sure I remembered the layout of the place but thought I could get us there then get directions if we got turned around inside. Foxwoods had more than doubled in size since the last time we had gone. John and Jean's sister Barbara were visiting for the weekend and they left with us but in separate cars just in case we had to leave if things were too emotional and Jean had to leave. I wanted to be sure we could plan our day if we needed to. They understood.

We arrived a little past twelve and were unable to park in valet so we parked in a large garage. We had already lost John and Barbara, so we called them and told them we'd catch up later. They were fine with that.

As we entered the casino my worst fears came true. The casino had changed markedly since the last time I had been there. We entered and immediately felt a bit lost. I asked for directions to the Rainmaker statue and we were on our way. We walked for a few minutes and then found ourselves standing by the tree next to the statue that this casino is named for, the Rainmaker.

I called Paula's cell and she directed us the remaining few feet. Then, as we were walking up the few short stairs, a blond woman met us. It was Paula and we all knew as soon as our eyes met that we were standing face to face with each other. We were right there with Drew's mother. All the months of waiting were behind us and we were excited to know we were going to get the chance to know all we could about Drew, Paula and the kind and generous family that made Jean's heart transplantation a reality.

I shook hands with Paula and introduced Jean. After a few pleasantries were exchanged although what they were I could not recall, as my mind was whirring away wondering what we would be experiencing in the next few minutes. We went to a table where Ron was introduced to us and the bonding began.

It was apparent right away that Paula and Jean would hit it off. To both their credits they reached out instantly to be sure there was no strangeness, awkwardness or discomfort. Paula and Jean got right down to the business at hand—finding out the circumstances of Drew's life that made it possible for him to donate and being able to thank her in person for a sacrifice that we knew must have been torment.

Chapter 8 - Meet Drew

Drew Doucet, Jean's donor,
photo courtesy of Paula, his mother

"I am your child
Wherever you go, you take me, too
Whatever I know, I learn from you
Whatever I do, you taught me to do
I am your child ... I am your hope,
I am your chance,
I am your child
Whatever I am, you taught me to be
I am your hope,
I am your chance,
I am your child."

Excerpted from *I Am Your Child* in memory of Drew
Doucet, written by Barry Manilow

Paula divulged to us that her son, Drew, whose middle name was Joseph, was born prematurely weighing less than two pounds when he was born. Doctors told Paula that Drew would not live very long. Indeed, he experienced 31 surgeries in his young life but defied the doctors and the odds by living for 21 years. He gave Paula and his siblings, Jared and Hayley, great joy. He was loving and wonderful. He had cerebral palsy and was speechless, but was quite able to communicate his wants, wishes and needs. He was a special needs student equipped with a speech device and was able to communicate even without a voice. He was a lovely young man who was able to help others to feel his love and warmth. My intuition was correct; Drew was like so many of the children whose lives I was privileged to intersect in my earlier work. I have come to think that even though I never met Drew, I knew him. I understood his world and his experiences from the collective experiences I had with so many families I worked with over the years. I held parents' hands when desperation struck them. I cried with them when they hurt or their child was mocked, was isolated, was ostracized, or when services were denied, when opportunities were not made available to their child. I tried to lift them when they were down and tried to generate hope when it seemed lost.

I think it is a great and wonderful irony that someone with Drew's disabilities was Jean's donor. I spent 27 years of my career working with and for people with disabilities, particularly newborn to three year-olds, advocating for them to get the services and equipment they needed. I think that God's fingerprints are all over this. I never expected much from my work in a monetary or individual way. I enjoyed the fulfillment of the work despite the staggering odds at times, and got plenty of reward in a more important way. I was doing work I loved and that was enough for me. But, I think perhaps I was given this wonderful gift, Jean's second chance at life, from Drew, who was like so many of the children I loved serving over the years. I sensed myself that what work I had done with children just like Drew all those years before had been brought full circle in a way that defied explanation. Coincidence? Perhaps. But I won't give in to that easy explanation. Symmetry; perfect symmetry. Maybe God's plan? I don't know the answer to that, but I will not quibble with it either.

It was the children, Jared and Hayley, Paula told us, who were the ones who made the point that Drew's organs should be donated because he would have wanted to give to others. He was very loving and thoughtful; they insisted he would want to express his love this way. She was hesitant to donate, but the children argued in favor and she relented. So, once again I am convinced of the goodness of children and young people. They seem to "get it."

We spent three and one half hours with Paula and Ron. In that time, we laughed; we wept; held each other's hands for comfort. We got lost in the chitchat; but when it came time to do what we had come to do Jean asked Paula if she wanted to feel Drew's heart beating in her chest. I was amazed that my beloved Jean, quiet, reserved, diffident and humble took the initiative sensing Paula's need to be reassured. Jean took Paula's hand and touched it lightly to her chest holding Paula's hand all the time it was there and they both shed tears and bonded on that spot in that moment, just as we had seen it happen in our mind's eye.

We learned that Drew was Paula's first child and that her bond to him was made even more special for the fight he put up to live through all his surgeries and all his special needs. He was very loving, tender and her "baby boy." He grew to be well over six feet tall although confined to a wheelchair all his life. It was impossible not to see the love she felt for him and how much his loss hurt her soul. But, she seemed delighted that someone like Jean had gotten Drew's heart. We told her how much it meant to us, inadequately in the way words often are, and we agreed to get together again, soon. We told her we wanted to meet her children and Drew's grandparents as well. When we asked Paula to show us a picture of Drew, she had forgotten to bring one in her haste to get to Foxwoods to meet us. She said she would send us her favorite picture of Drew when she got home.

Not long after we met, a package arrived from Paula containing a framed photograph of a handsome blond young man sitting is his wheelchair looking so full of life and beauty while on a boat out on the water. (The photo that is shown above.) His picture is now next to Paula's gift, a Willow Tree figurine of a little boy holding a heart that sits on our bookcase in our family room. Right where it belongs, with the pictures of our grandsons and other family members. Drew is one of us now and forever more.

And ironically, we learned that Paula works at a private club named the *St. Jean Club*! The church in Amesbury is called All Saints. The day Jean received her transplanted heart was All Saints Day in the Catholic liturgical calendar, November 1st. The church was the result of a merger of two churches, one of which was formerly St. Joseph. *Joseph.* My father's name; my name; our son's name; our grandson's middle name and Drew's middle name. Mere coincidence? Maybe. But, you'll have a hard time convincing us it is only that.

There are far too many mysterious and even mystical events that we fail to comprehend. I have tried to figure this out in some rational and reasoning way. There are times when I can. Other times, I simply revert to the knowledge that some things are just mystifying. And, that's all right, too.

And for all this, we give our *heartfelt* thanks each and every day. That is so simple to understand.

Chapter 9 - Jean's First Person Account of What Led Up to Her Transplant

Author's Note: This chapter is offered as insight into the way women are sometimes treated when they present conditions that may be or lead to heart disease. We do not do so to castigate or criticize but to offer this as a caution to women readers. Know your body and learn how illness in women is different from illness in men. Too often, women are misdiagnosed or their symptoms are lightly regarded, disregarded or taken less seriously. Recently, greater awareness of women's heart health has led to changes in the way medicine responds to women's heart health issues. We are glad of that.

When Joe succumbed to the encouragement to write *Heartfelt*, I knew that I would have to write something. I am not a writer, nor someone easily able to express myself publicly. I was anxious because, although I was at the center of this, I was also out of the loop for much of the day, November 1st, 2007, when all heck was breaking loose. That's a strange disconnection for me but in reality, because I was the recipient, I was sedated for much of that day and much of what transpired did so without my being consciously aware. Of course, leading up to the day of my transplant, I was fully there. The website and Joe's dedication to it, keeping everyone informed chronicles the entire event so there is not much more I can add to that. I can, however, say what my perspective was and is now. Despite my reluctance to write, here I am writing. Anything *is* possible.

I first learned I had heart disease almost by accident it seemed. For so many years, my doctors treated my symptoms: tachycardia, arrhythmia, mitral valve prolapse as something that was bothersome, unsettling, but not *heart disease*. At the time, doctors were following conventional medical wisdom. Some doctors I saw thought my symptoms were stress related; others thought they were psychological; still others seemed to think I was just a hysterical woman. In the deepest recesses of my mind, I knew, intuitively, something was wrong. After many years of trying to get a handle on this and to get a clear diagnosis, I resigned myself to a life filled with doubt, fear and uncertainty. I became a cardiac neurotic all right. I spent every day of my life afraid, paralyzed by the thought that there was something very wrong with me, never assured it would be fixable. I was in the end, happily wrong in the most profound way. But all those years of being afraid had taken their toll on me. I had become pretty fatalistic.

Years later I went to see my primary care physician in Connecticut around 2002. He heard something he didn't like the sound of when he listened to my heart. He performed a cardiogram, which showed different results from earlier cardiograms. He was alarmed and so was I based on his demeanor and reaction. Joe was sitting in the waiting room when the doctor went out to tell him that I was to go to Yale immediately. I went to Yale-New Haven Hospital by ambulance directly from his office. This was the beginning of many rides to come to the hospital in ambulances over the next few years. That day is where this saga began in earnest. For the first time, really, I was being seen for heart disease, real, not imagined. Eight years later, I am alive, writing this and forever grateful to Drew, Paula, Jared and Hayley.

From that day forward, I was under the constant care of the Yale Cardiology group whose fine cardiologists, principally Dr. Joe Brennan and Dr. Jude Clancy, along with others in the group, began the work that eventually led to more concerted care of my heart. Their skill, their technologies and their caring carried me through all the procedures. I experienced scans, stress tests, injections of dye, ultra sounds, catheterizations, stents and all the assorted array of what modern medicine can offer. I was getting better care but my health was becoming impaired despite their best efforts and the use of the newest technology medicine had to offer.

In the early going I never fully realized that I was on the path to transplantation. In my doctors' efforts to get my heart condition under control, I first received a pacemaker that worked to keep my heart beating properly so that my heart rhythm would be consistent, not like my skipping heartbeats had been. A few years later, when that device was unable to keep up with the continuing decline of my heart function, I had a pacemaker/stimulator implanted. That worked for a few years until my heart regressed to a worsened state and I needed a pacemaker/stimulator/defibrillator implanted that assured me that my heart would not stop beating in the event I experienced a heart attack or if my heart went into fibrillation, a more likely event because of my heart's inefficiency. It was at this point I fully understood my heart was getting weaker and weaker and I began to despair that my life would be short. After experiencing two seizures in a few minutes' time when the defibrillator fired in 2007, I was told that I would have to receive a new heart! That was August 2007. I had heard the word transplant mentioned years before, but never in my wildest imagination did I ever think it was really an option. How realistic was that? My brother died in 2006 from a heart condition not too unlike mine; he was thought to be a transplant candidate but was unable to live long enough to get one when it was discovered that his aorta was calcified and sewing a new heart into him would be impossible. That thought lingered in my mind, too. My fear was well grounded, I thought.

After a visit to the ER when the defibrillator fired twice in August 2007, I was scheduled to see the Yale Cardiology doctors again. I had an echocardiogram done again. Following the test, Dr. Brennan informed me I had only a ten percent heart function. I knew there was bad news coming before he spoke when I saw his face as he walked into the examination room. We had a very cordial relationship and close bond that developed over the years, so I read his emotions right there on his face. I knew! Leaving the cardiology group office that day, I wondered where this was headed and I was sure my life was soon going to end. It was a week before my sixtieth birthday. As Joe and I left the parking lot, we barely spoke, both of us pondering what lay ahead. It was a terrifying day, but then things got even more dramatic very quickly.

My heart was performing only minimally, not enough to keep me alive. That day I was told that I needed a transplant and I would be put on the transplant list; the work up procedures began immediately. Within days, I started with blood work and urinalysis and output studies to see how my kidneys were functioning. On September 24th, while I was at work, I received a call from Yale instructing me to call an ambulance and get myself to Yale-Hew Haven Hospital immediately where the other procedures would be performed. The results so far were not good and I was failing even more quickly than expected. I was retaining too much fluid because my heart was so inefficient and my kidneys were not adequately excreting fluids from my body so that I was in jeopardy of heart failure, drowning in my own body fluids. I was run through more tests after being admitted to the ER then to the Cardiac Care Unit, more tests that one can imagine. From that night onward, I felt like I was in a dream hoping to awake from this where everything would be all right. I guess I was in denial that my life was about to change radically. I had no idea what the next steps would be. In just a few short weeks I would know. But that night the wait for a new heart began in earnest. My doctors told me that I could not leave the hospital without a new heart. My fate was sealed. Now, I was in the fight of my life and was helpless to do anything about it. From here on out, I was either going to die waiting for a heart or get one and going on with my life. It was clearly out of my hands. There was nothing I could do to directly affect the outcome. I was literally at the mercy of outside forces, chance and random occurrences, God, to keep me alive. I was scared like I had never before been scared. Yet, I found calmness during the turmoil. I can't be certain why that is. But being hospitalized for so long was a new experience, one I had no way to prepare for. I prayed hoping that God would bring me either the new heart I needed, or that I would be okay with dying. Afraid yet hopeful. Scared but resigned. Lonely but not alone. Uncomfortable but comforted. Ambivalent but certain. All these emotions ran through me in waves and on some days, I vacillated wildly between those polar contradictions.

The days dragged on to weeks; September quickly turned into October. Then November was looming. I was becoming depressed, very depressed. I walked the halls every day to keep my strength and spirits up, sometimes with Joe at my side, but often as not I walked with a new friend. While walking I met another woman waiting for a transplant. Her name was Frenchie. Her strength and positive attitude really helped to keep me going when the darker moments arrived. She made everyone on the unit laugh and kept all of us upbeat. Her outlook was infectious. I needed that; alone I was despairing, with her help I had hope. I told Joe I had a dream, a premonition really that if I got a heart, it would be a Thursday. I can't explain this, but it was a strong sense. I am not a superstitious person, but for some reason this experience made me realize that I was hoping and as long as I had hope, I had a chance to survive. After six long weeks the doctors came to my bedside on *Thursday*, (my premonition was a foretelling after all) November 1st, 2007 and announced that they had a heart. A transplant team doctor was going to Massachusetts to examine it and; if it was a good heart, pick it up and take it to Yale. The blood type and tissue matches were all good they said. At that moment, I realized, I finally knew for certain, this could turn out one way or another but I was going to get a new heart. No guarantees, but a chance. I have never been so scared in my life. I called home, spoke to my son Chris and told him to get Joe on the phone. When Joe answered I blurted out, "They have a heart." He said he would race right to the hospital. It is a 40-mile trip, so I knew he wouldn't be there soon. Meantime, my room and the unit began to buzz. Word gets around fast on a unit like this. Everyone is pulling for one another. You hear people cheering and clapping. The level of intensity seems to pick up. I guess it is like the time just before kickoff of a football game, when everyone knows that in a few moments, there will be a lot of excitement. There were three of us waiting for hearts: Frenchie, Tony and me. I had been there the longest although Frenchie might have been admitted around the same time. We were all friends by this time, each of us pulling for the other, no competition, just wanting to see each other get a shot at life.

Shortly after Joe and Chris arrived, I found myself surrounded by so many doctors and nurses it became a blur. My regular cardiologists Dr. Brennan and Dr. Clancy, who had treated me before I became a transplant candidate, came by to wish me luck, shake my hand, kiss me and reassure me. Somehow they had heard at the hospital that morning that I was getting prepped for a new heart. The room became a madhouse of activity awaiting a gurney, seeing it arrive with an orderly who placed me on it. Joe held my hand; Chris and Joe kissed me good-bye, although I was not certain at that moment if it was a temporary or final good bye. I wish I could remember more from this point on, but at 11:20 AM, I was being wheeled down to the OR to wait and be prepped.

I had no way of knowing if I would ever wake from this. As I lay there in the OR waiting for the heart to arrive, I remember a young medical student who was there holding my hand and talking so positively about what was going to take place. He gave me so much courage and faith. That was one of the things I remember before I went under anesthesia. I never did get his name, but I owe him so much. I don't know if I could have been as calm in my fearful state had he not taken such care of my emotions and soothing me. No one I loved was anywhere near me;

I was as alone and in the company of strangers, but he made me feel calmer and for him, I am so thankful. As the time drew closer all I could think of was, "Will it be a go or not?" "Will I make it or not?" The very last recollection I have was someone telling me that there was a chance that when the heart arrived and the surgeons opened my chest, there was still a chance that the surgery, for any number of reasons, might not happen and they might have to close me without the transplant. I could wake up tomorrow and still have my own heart. I told Pat the OR nurse, to tell Joe that if I survived the surgery, I was going to shop till I dropped. Then, silence.

When I awoke on November 2nd, having lost much of a full day, I could not move my limbs. That scared me. But when one of my nurses removed me from the respirator I had been on since I came out of surgery, I began to get feeling back in my limbs. All was fine and I was able to move again. My new heart was beating strongly and I was alive. *I knew I had made it!*

Then it struck me. I realized that I was alive only because someone else had died. I asked Joe in a hushed voice, I still was unable to speak because of the respirator's effect, "Whose heart do I have?" When he told me it was from a 21 year-old man, I wept quietly and said in a whisper, "That poor mother."

Chapter 10 - The Children's Reflections

Author's Note: When a loved one goes through transplantation, the entire family goes through it with the one in surgery. Each of us senses, perceives and feels emotions based on our own interpretation of the experience from inside ourselves. In an effort to assist family members, we offer our children's input to show the range of both experiences and emotions that are felt as this life changing experience occurs. Our children are grown, all adults. Three lived in Colorado when Jean was hospitalized, One, Chris was with us at the time but has since moved to Phoenix where he lives and works. He is the only one of the children physically present at his mother's bedside the weeks leading up to and the day of the transplant. Stacie, Joe and Amy all traveled to Jean's side from their homes in Colorado to share the experience with us. How they shared it with one another, neither Jean nor I know for certain as we were not there with them. Having raised them, we know they held onto one another for support.

Stacie's Impressions

It's one of those moments you know you will never forget. Mom called and at some point in the conversation she said pretty matter-of-factly that the doctor told her she would need a heart transplant. I'm sorry, what did you just say? A what? Had I heard her correctly? Not bypass surgery, not an angioplasty, not diuretics to get the fluid off, not a change in eating/lifestyle habits, but a heart transplant. Wow! What do you say? Oh my God.

At this point, mom was still at home and living life, as she knew it. Just after I got off the phone it dawned on me that I knew that at some point we would be faced with the severity of her illness. Then it hit me, I was not ready to lose my mother. Not that you ever are, but she was so young, had four grandson's who adored her, four children who still needed their mother. It just wasn't her time. I cried like a baby as my husband tried to comfort me. It was a lot to take in. If it was a lot for me, what must mom be going through?

At the time when she was admitted to the hospital and we learned she would not leave without a new heart, everything changed. My siblings and I discussed how we could help them through this. Early fall I took a trip by myself to spend some time with mom at the hospital.

Upon entering her hospital room in the ICU, I found her much thinner, but in good spirits, despite the multiple wires and tubes restricting her movements. Being a nurse, none of that surprised me. I had ICU experience and could understand all that. But knowing that this was her home until a heart became available…then the questions: how long, what if one doesn't come soon enough?

We made the best of it. I gave her a pedicure, got her hair cut, brought candy, visited with well wishers, caught up on TV, snuck in a piece of pizza, and just hung with mom. It wasn't bad if you didn't think of the severity of the situation.

One morning dad dropped me off at the hospital on his way to the university. I entered to find my mom sitting in the chair. She looked good. I sat on the bed only to hear her ask me to get out some paper ... she wanted to plan her funeral service. Not exactly the plan I had for my day, but how do you say no to that? So I told her I would write it down only because we would *not* need it. I joked it would be an exercise in warding off the evil spirits.

She told me where the services were to be held, but she was most concerned about the food, an Italian trait. And Italian it was to be ... catered by one of her favorite restaurants. Although I typed up the details, I don't remember them now. I do remember how hard that was to do with my mother, but how important it was for her to have it planned so dad wouldn't have to worry. I told my dad of this conversation that night on our ride to his home. I think he was upset not to be privy to it, but I told him I thought it would have been much more difficult for mom to have to discuss those arrangements with him, her husband of almost forty years. He was her biggest fan, her positive force. He never let on if he ever had a doubt that a heart might not become available. He was a rock, most of the time.

One night on the way home we stopped for a bite at the Hideaway, their favorite local bar. My brother Chris joined us. We talked about mom and how she was doing and my father finally broke down. He cried like I've never seen him cry and I knew this was taking a toll on him. But I think it helped to get it out, have family surrounding and supporting him. It's never easy for a daughter to see her father cry, but I think he needed to just let it go.

As I prepared to return home to my family, I said "good-bye" to my mother, not really thinking that it could really be the last time. I held on to hope. The time she had spent in the ICU prepared her body for the transplant. I believe she would not have survived had a heart become available shortly after being hospitalized. She needed that time to get rid of the fluid accumulation, let her organs rest and prepare for the journey that lie ahead.

On November 1st, I got a text message from dad saying, "the Eagle has landed." A heart from the Boston area appeared to be a match. I was on my way to work and felt anxious. After two false alarms, could this really be it? God, I hoped so. As hopeful as I was, I knew that I was not the only one thinking about the person that lost a life just the day before. It's difficult to know that someone had to die to give my mom life. I prayed with my children for both mom and the family of the boy who donated his heart. I was so thankful for the decision to donate his organs.

I took a chance and called my mom's cell phone mid-morning and had a brief chance to speak to her just before they took her to surgery. All the requirements for a match looked great. I told her that she was strong, she would get through this and that I loved her. She was crying on the other end of the line. After hanging up, I broke down with a co-worker, who said the most amazing prayer with me. Asking for the Lord to guide the surgeon's hands as he gave my mother a new chance at life, I was touched by her words. And just like another day at the office for a cardiac surgeon, mom sailed through her surgery with flying colors. I found it amazing to learn that the surgeon told dad it was easier to perform a transplant than to perform bypass surgery! Who would have thought?

My siblings and I took turns traveling East after mom's transplant. My sister was fortunate to be there the morning she woke up. I was to arrive in time to take her home. I took the overnight flight from Denver to Hartford and arrived at the hospital very early. I found my way to mom's room, pushed open the door, and saw her—so small and frail, and trembling in her sleep. I just watched her for a few minutes, taking in the fact that she was here, alive, sleeping, breathing, with the heart of anotherbeating in her chest.

I sat at her bedside for a while trying not to wake her. After some time, she stirred and said "Hi Stac." As if she had seen me just the day before, she was greeting me as she often had. What a blessing to hear her speak, and sound just like herself. She was still recovering from the surgery, still having some pain, still gaining strength to prepare for her discharge home the next day, not even two weeks after the heart transplant.

I arrived the next day to bring her home. I met with the transplant coordinator and the social worker to go over the binder of instructions for mom's medications and monitoring. This was going to be work and she seemed so frail. I told her I would get all of her medications sorted into a system that she and dad could easily follow and duplicate.

We took the drive home with a stop to get a bite to eat. That's my mom, on them mend, and wanting to go to a restaurant for lunch. Who was I to tell her no after six weeks in the hospital? Upon arrival at the house, she walked in to find a banner welcoming her home, made by Chris' girlfriend, Alia. Flowers were on the table, cards everywhere. And here was mom walking ever so slowly around her house as if seeing it for the first time, or taking in what she thought she might have never seen again.

The first year was not an easy one for mom. However, by medical standards, she soared through it with flying colors. She never had to be hospitalized for signs of rejection, common after transplants. All her blood work and test results were promising. She went to cardiac rehab and gained strength that she desperately needed just to get up by herself, or step on the curb without falling. I know it was difficult for her and I also know she was grateful to be alive.

My sister Amy took the lead to form a team for the Colorado Donor Dash in 2008. She fittingly called it "Team Jean." We walked in support of organ donors and recipients alike. It was a beautiful tribute for a great cause.

I was hoping that mom and dad would hear back from the donor family at some point. I couldn't imagine mom not knowing where the heart came from. I also respected that it might be difficult for the donor family to meet the recipient. However, after months of communication through proper anonymous channels, mom went on not only to learn the name of the donor, but to meet his mother. A few months after meeting Paula Flint and learning about her son Drew, mom and dad made a trip to Amesbury, MA to meet the rest of the family, and the press. It was a very emotional weekend for mom. A time to share; to remember; to reflect; to rejoice, and to say thank you. The decision of Drew's family brought two families together.

This year we have added new members to "Team Jean 2009," including Paula Flint, her daughter and some of their friends. I look forward to meeting them and know that saying thank you could never be enough. I am forever grateful for their decision in the face of grief. I am thankful to have my mother for whatever time God sees fit.

Amy's View

The summer of 2007 would prove to be the most difficult summer I have yet to endure in my adulthood. At a family reunion in Cape Cod in June, it was apparent that my mother's congestive heart failure was gaining speed and her body was losing the struggle. She appeared very ashen, her extremities were very swollen, and she was admitted to the hospital on Cape Cod to remove some of the fluid that had developed around her lungs while we were there. It was returning from the family reunion that the true test of all of us in the family would begin, both as individuals and collectively.

As the summer began to wear on, there were worsening reports on my mother's health from the East coast. Knowing that congestive heart failure is a progressive disease, the local family (my brother Joe, sister Stacie and I) began to discuss what the next "steps" would be for her and for us. The outlook seemed very grim.

In September, my mother was admitted to the hospital for what would become her "final" hospitalization. The physicians told us that my mother would probably never leave the hospital, that her disease had progressed to the point where no medicines or therapies could relieve her heart any more. It was a very sad and anxious time for all of us since we didn't know what to expect (except for the worst) with each passing day. It seemed phone calls would deepen everyone's level of anxiety as the days wore on.

My sister Stacie took a trip to be with my mom for a week while she was in the hospital. Her reports were never much good news as my mom continued to become weaker and more tired. My brother Joe and I had started to discuss when we would go to spend some last moments with our mother.

It was amidst all of this, the transplant team stepped in at Yale-New Haven Hospital to evaluate whether or not mom would qualify for a heart transplant. I, personally, had my own doubts that this was a possibility for my mother for a number of reasons. I had completed two transplant rotations while in pharmacy school and I suspected her chances were not the best. It was while waiting to hear the "verdict" from the transplant team that I began to brace myself for the time that my mother would leave this world and started to think about what life was going to look like without her. It was a very emotional time.

To all of our surprises, mom qualified for a transplant and was then placed on the top of the transplant list as by this point, her condition merited her being moved up quickly. We were surprised by the news and this is when hope stepped in to compete with the sea of all the other swirling emotions to deal with from day to day. The team at Yale told us to expect around two weeks to get a heart once placed at the top of the list so with this information, we waited our time … two weeks went by, no heart for mom. There were a few close matches but nothing doing. We still had hope that a heart would come soon. In the meantime, my siblings and I decided that it would work out best for all of our schedules if I could be there immediately post-surgery to be with mom. One of us had to be. I began to make tentative arrangements. Week three went by without a sign of a donor and it was then that I began to get worried. Where once there was hope, now sat uncertainty and some despair. The days leading up to November 1st were no different.

I received a phone call early on November 1st that a heart from Massachusetts was available and that my mother would be rushed to surgery very soon. I was overcome with fear and so many questions: "what if she doesn't make it through the surgery?" "What if the heart doesn't beat once it's in there?" "What if? ... What if? ... What if I never get the chance to speak to my mother again?" I frantically tried to reach my mom on her cell phone. I heard her voice on the other line and in that moment, I had no idea what to say! I sobbed and she was sobbing too. I asked, "Are you scared, mom?" She replied, "Yes." I tried to offer some encouraging words as best I could and made sure she heard me say that I loved her and I would be there when she woke up. All I could do for the next hour was sob and pray that everything would work out, as it should. I think that was the longest day of my life.

We received periodic updates from my father all day about her progress. Each text message or e-mail reported nothing but good news: "new heart is in," "new heart is beating," "surgeons are wrapping up and all signs look good." I was elated by the news and knew that this must have been the hardest day of my father's life as well. This entire experience was a lot for him to have to endure, understandably. I took a red-eye flight and got into Connecticut at 5 AM the next morning. I was anxious to get to the hospital. I met up with my father and off we went to Yale. Dad tried to forewarn me that mom looked dreadful and that I should brace myself for the sight of her looking near death.

When we arrived at the hospital it was around 7AM The nursing team told us that we could both go to see her but for no more than 15 minutes every hour as she was still in a critical recovery period. We hurried to her room.

When we got there, my father and I each took a side of the bed. My mother had her eyes closed and she looked to be resting peacefully in spite of the ventilator in her throat, the 12 or so IV bags attached to her body, her swollen and bruised neck, and all the pain she must have been in. I was startled by how bruised her neck and chest looked as I had never seen this type of surgery before. The color in her face was not the ashen color from the summer but a healthy bronze, almost as if she had a suntan. She had a long cut down her sternum that was now stapled closed. We both took her hands and she awoke. She seemed startled to see me; and all I could say was, "I told you I would be here when you woke up." She acknowledged my words with her eyes. She then looked at my father and pointed to her heart trying to ask, "Whose heart did I get?" He told her all we knew was that it came from a twenty-one year old man. My mom began to get choked up and cry. She mouthed the words, "That poor mother." We urged her not to think about such upsetting things now but to focus on her recovery. I continued to sit there for the remainder of the short time and held her hand. I cried and was in disbelief of the magnitude of what this experience was going to be for my family. I knew my mother had a very long and difficult recovery after she was to leave the hospital. It was so hard to take it all in. But she didn't look as bad a Dad reported she had looked the previous night. He was amazed at how quickly she had improved in just the few hours since he had seen her last.

My father and I complied with the "every 15 minutes per hour rule" and went in each hour for our turns to be with her. As the day went on, her physical recovery was extraordinary to watch! Each time I went in, at least one IV bag had been removed, the bruising was quickly fading, and she was sitting up in bed! At some point early on, she was taken off the ventilator, around mid-morning. I knew I was witnessing medicine at its finest. True to form, my mother was talking and making jokes once she could breathe on her own! The rest of the day was just about getting her to make small steps: eating a little and sipping a little water or carbonated beverages in an attempt to get her stomach to "wake up" and start to function normally again. She made wonderful strides in that very first day alone! I was so thankful I came to be with her and my dad and so shared my day with my siblings and friends by e-mails and phone calls. What a day it was for all us! We couldn't help but remember that where we had so much joy, another family must be reeling in pain and sorrow. All of this would sort itself out in time I knew. As my father and I drove away from the hospital that first night, I witnessed the most stunning sunset I had ever seen and I knew that a miracle happened today. God had truly blessed us with the beauty of all that is good in the world. That sunset sealed the day perfectly—glory and hope.

The rest of my trip was spent helping out my dad around the house and our daylong trips to see my mom. There were many doctor visits and questions about therapies and such. I was with her when the doctors removed her chest tube and got to witness all the additional milestones she had to tackle in her recovery. I felt so lucky to be there and I was exceedingly proud of my mother's will and courage to make it through all of this. Leaving a few short days later was one of the hardest things I had ever had to do!

My brother and sister both made trips out to be with my mom upon her departure from the hospital and back into life, as she once knew it. The first month at home was very complicated for my mom, as she had to adhere to strict daily regimens from the transplant team so that they could continue to evaluate her recovery while away from the hospital. She also had to endure weekly heart biopsies, which were stressful and painful for her. I returned to aid in the recovery efforts in December for a week and again was able to witness the wonderful strides made by my mother in her recovery. It was slow but sure.

I vowed after this experience that I would always honor and treasure the young man that gave up his life and whose family gave his heart to my mother and in doing so, gave us all the blessing of more time and life together. After the New Year, there was some initial contact with the donor family and as the year went on, plans were made so my mom and dad could meet the young man's (named Drew) mother, Paula. It was quite an emotional experience for all of us, especially my mother and father, understandably. Here in Colorado, we spoke of when we could possibly meet them and what that must have been like for all of them. In our own hearts, we shared in the experience.

I decided the best way to celebrate Drew, his family, and my mother was to participate in the Donor Dash, a fund-raising walk to increase organ donation awareness here in Denver. It has become an annual event. Our team is named *Team Jean* and this will be our second year walking in the race. Last year, our first race, we still didn't know who the donor was but this year will be very different! We are blessed to have Paula, Drew's siblings, and my mother and father joining us for this year's race in a few weeks!

Our team has grown in size as we have offered this tribute to our friends to share with us.

Now that all the immediate stress of the transplant is over, my mother is in great health, and we know the donor's family, we can join our families together as they should be. I am expecting an emotional meeting for all of us and one that we are ready to have. What will I say? "Thank you?" "Sorry for your loss?" Words escape me but the emotions don't. Maybe a hug with Drew's mom will be all the "words" I will need to say.

Please be an organ and tissue donor after all. You can't take anything with you when you go!

Joe's View

Although we were all involved in the events leading up to our mom's heart transplant, our involvement was not the same due to our proximity and perceptions of what was taking place. We knew our mom's cardiac health had begun to deteriorate over the years, as holiday excitement was often replaced by visits to the ER. When I was told that my mom was in the hospital and would remain there until she received a heart transplant. I started questioning how many days we'd have left with our mother. Although I'm not a healthcare practitioner by any stretch of the imagination, I have spent a lot of time around the organ and tissue transplant professional community and understood the gravity of needing an organ to survive. How many days/months could mom go on in her condition and would there be a donor with the right blood type, who had a healthy heart that could be successfully transplanted? The odds were staggering.

As the weeks leading up to the heart transplant progressed, my mom's attitude and overall health seemed to improve, as she had been closely monitored in the hospital in order to stabilize her and prepare her for a transplant—should a heart become available. I know the stress and uncertainty became unbearable at times, but her patience and will to survive were always present. My dad, on the other hand, started to show signs of fatigue and despair, as the daily commutes to the hospital and the long days began to wear him down. The occasional false alarm that there was a heart available from a viable donor only added to the anxiety and, ultimately, disappointment.

As days turned into weeks, I started wondering how long this was going to last and whether or not my mom was going to get the heart she so desperately needed. When my dad called and said that a young man's heart had become available and the blood types matched, I was on pins and needles. We all knew how serious this surgery was going to be—to have to successfully take someone's heart and transplant it into our mom. Could she endure a surgical procedure that was this invasive? Would her immune system reject her newly transplanted heart or would she regain her strength and health and continue to live a healthy and happy life? All we could do was pray that everything would be successful.

I was fortunate enough to get to Connecticut just a few days after my mom's procedure and was blown away at how good she looked. Although she wasn't out of the woods by any stretch of the imagination, her color looked great and she seemed to regain a little strength each day that passed. The doctors and staff at the hospital stayed on top of her medication regimen and began to plan for her discharge. All those months of uncertainty, worry, and despair seemed to be a thing of the past as mom and dad began to focus on the healthy days ahead. I know my mom was eager to get out of the hospital after spending six weeks there, and my dad was equally excited to have her home so they could get their life and relationship back on track. It was great to spend time with my parents and to see them not just as "mom and dad" but as fellow human beings who are able to endure pain and suffering with poise, composure, and hope.

For me, the most impressive aspect of the transplant cannot be summarized in just a few short paragraphs. As I mentioned earlier, I've had the honor to be involved in organ and tissue donation and transplantation through my ex-wife's career in the industry. What amazes me more than anything is the fact that a donor family, when confronted with something as traumatic as an unexpected loss of a loved one, can make the heart-wrenching decision to donate organs to a total stranger. Furthermore, science and medical technology (and divine intervention) all come together to ensure that organs are successfully removed and transplanted into another human being. Amazing!

I truly cannot elaborate on all the great things that I've witnessed as a result of my mom's transplant. I've seen what "true love" is through my dad's commitment to my mom's health and well being. I've witnessed my mom's strength, courage, and determination—not to just survive but also thrive. Our relationships within our family have been strengthened on so many levels as a result of my mom's experience. I have seen new friendships begin between our family and Drew's family—friendships that have been forged as a result of love, compassion, and selfless acts of kindness toward total strangers. All in all, I have had the privilege to see what love means on so many levels and how, as human beings, we are all interconnected as a species even though we oftentimes fail to recognize that. To quote Anon, "Man must live by faith—faith in himself, and faith in others." It's amazing to think of my mom's journey and everything she's had to endure and overcome to get to where she is today. Quite honestly, she is the only one who can truly elaborate on the experience and the dramatic effect it has had on her life and how she now lives it.

Chris' View

I always thought I had intuition so I was not in any way scared or concerned about the outcome of what mom had in front of her when God sent the heart to us because I had a sense that things would work out for her. The donor heart was already identified as a suitable match, and even if mom were to perish from surgery, post-op complications or rejection, at least she had been given an opportunity for a rebirth. Not many families are blessed by the medical technology available today or have access to the skills of today's doctors to bring new life. But without donors, who give life when least expected, none of this is possible.

I knew my mom was frightened to death as was as my dad, and for good reason. I somehow sensed that the medical staff at Yale, God, and our family's strength and positive outlook would make it all happen. I was more frightened of the fact that my dad once joked years earlier and in happier times, when mom was still healthy, about moving in with me if mom ever passed away. That struck more fear in me than mom's surgery. (I joke about that now, but there was a time when the thought of dad's moving in with me was a bit unnerving until mom got really sick, that is.) On a serious note, in the years leading up to the transplant, we were all watching mom die in front of our eyes. We could see it in her face, in her swollen body, and her general aura was dwindling as time passed. In my view, watching mom slipping away was more frightening to see than the thought of her having her chest opened and a donor heart being placed in her body. I liked her chances in the transplant over knowing what she was going through with her failing heart.

When the day was over, I was happy that my dad might actually get his wife back in one piece, that I had mom back in one piece, and that we all shared this strange, stressful but bonding time together. I had buried some friends, most very young, so I was more prepared perhaps than my siblings were to think about burying one of my parents. I wasn't sure if my brother and sisters were ready or equipped to handle such a tragedy and I think that my dad would have been so distraught over mom's passing that it might have shortened his life as well. That preyed on my mind as I watched the events of the day unfold while sitting in the waiting room with my dad.

I know that I'm blessed to have my family. Dad and mom are the greatest, so great that if and when their time comes, I won't mourn their deaths as much as I will celebrate their lives and the lives that they both have changed. I believe we don't truly die; we simply shed our bodies and that's nothing to fear; it's something to embrace and so I was embracing any outcome. Of course, I am happy for the one we got. And, I prayed that day knowing that everything would be all right. Still, I wanted to be absolutely sure that mom came through it. When the OR nurse called my dad to tell him mom's transplant was done and the heart was beating, we both breathed a sigh of relief and shed tears of joy and release, hugging each other as we soaked in the news. Strangers in the waiting room cheered and applauded our great news. That was quite a sight when you consider that everyone in that room is waiting to hear some news about their own loved ones, yet they found the power to cheer for us.

Shortly after mom came home, in time for Thanksgiving 2007, I made plans to relocate to Phoenix. By Christmas Day, when I left, I knew mom was improving daily and on her way toward full recovery despite the ups and downs she had experienced. I left that day with full confidence that she would be fine and she and dad would continue to build their lives anew.

Chapter 11 - Going Public and Serving the Cause

> "Love gave me confidence and adversity gave me purpose."
> Eunice Kennedy Shriver

Jean and I recognize we have been blessed beyond belief. In a way to give back, we have determined that we want to do as much as we can to spread the word about organ donation. In that effort, we have pledged the proceeds from the sales of *Heartfelt* to Donate Life and UNOS, but also to take *Heartfelt* on a talking tour, if we can, meet with people to share Jean's and Drew's triumphant story and to trumpet the cause of organ donation wherever and whenever we can. We have already met with a representative of Donate Life in Connecticut and have begun to plan how best we can help. We will not rest until we have done what we can to assist those still waiting. These next few pages are offered to show that this effort is already underway as you will see. Meeting family members, visiting communities, interviewing with the press, all these efforts will be part of our efforts to give something back. We ask for your prayers and support;

hopeful that our work yields results that help you and your loved ones.

One of our first efforts at this was to travel In June 2009 to Drew's hometown of Amesbury MA to visit his family, meet his grandparents, his uncles and aunts and those great friends who supported Paula through her arduous time. We were delighted to have this opportunity. It gave us the sense that we could indeed be useful to people in urging them to look into donation and to see what can happen when we realize that we have so much to offer one another that we may never have thought of. We arrived late in the day on Friday, June 19th and met with the gang at the St. Jean Club. We were amazed at the support all around us. Signs on the wall, fund raising efforts to generate funds for Paula to participate in an event memorializing Drew and promoting organ donation. We met so many people we were dizzy trying to remember all their names (Cheryl, Gay, Patrice, Tammi, Courtney, Gino, and so many more) and were emotionally spent from all the hugs and kisses and handshakes as we were greeted as 'old friends', despite the fact we had never set foot in Amesbury or had ever met anyone in this place in our lives. But, this was just the beginning, as we were quick to find out.

The next day, June 20th, 2009, Jean and Paula were interviewed by the local newspaper and a TV station from Boston covering the story. This story was going public. Steve Jones, or "Jonesy" as Paula and Ron call him, had done all the groundwork getting this pulled together. He is not a professional public relations man, but he is a loyal and determined friend and supporter of Paula's who volunteered to get this day arranged. He was steadfast in his effort to see it through. We thank him for all that he made possible. Needless to say, this was a tough, emotionally raw day for everyone, as old wounds were once again reopened. Jean and Paula were interviewed to get the story out to the public. They were powerful, saying things that neither of them had prepared beforehand. They spoke from their hearts. Neither is especially accustomed to speaking publicly or calling attention to herself. Both are reserved, quiet and private people. And this was a deeply profound experience that brought our families together. But on this day what had brought us together made us all more public, more vulnerable, more emotional but, happily, more bonded. We think that the day was successful in that regard. If you would like to see these events go to http://www1.whdh.com/news/articles/local/BO116932/. In addition, the local newspaper, *The Daily News,* at www.newburyportmews.com ran a feature story entitled, "*His beats to keep me alive - heart donor's family meets woman whose life was saved,*" written by Jill Oestereicher Gross, dated June 25th, 2009. It was front-page news that day, dateline Amesbury MA. Local to be sure, but sent around the country by us and anyone else who wanted to spread the word.

So, we were now out in public where we believe the most good can come of this story of salvation, resurrection, love and hope. And, we now know that we can and must do this on behalf of others as a part of our way of paying it both forward and back.

Chapter 12 - A Word About Organ Donation

Each day thousands of people, infants, children and adults, lie in hospital rooms or wait at home throughout the United States and other countries hoping for an organ to *literally* save their lives. The organ donation miracles are stories that resonate around the world but too few of our brothers and sisters are saved. Each year more people die than are saved because there are not enough donors to assist all who need an organ. Because we have been blessed in our family, we know the value and mystery of this wonderful gift. We know now after meeting Paula, Jared and Hayley that Drew's donation saved five people —*five*—not just Jean. Imagine the gift that this is for all those who were saved by Drew.

We urge everyone who reads this book to consider organ donation. Talk about it as a family. Check off the box on your driver's license; put your decision in your living wills or end of life directives to guide your families to donate so that others can live on or simply get online and find the nearest organ donation agency in your area or region and sign up. Talk to your friends, to your clergyman, to anyone, who will be able to guide you should you have any reservations at all. Saving a life is the greatest gift anyone can give. All religions recognize this principle. All of us, whether we practice a religious faith or not, know intuitively that donating our organs, if they can help someone, is a selfless act of faith and hope. No one is "too young," "too old" or "too disabled" to be a donor. Each of us need only decide.

We wish that all stories like Jean's had the kind of happy ending we have had. Sadly, we know that is not at all the case. But if we all put our collective efforts into this, we can make a difference one donor at a time. Talk it up. It could save your life or the life of someone you love. Please be sure to educate yourself as best you can so that you can make informed decisions about this very important part of realizing how interconnected we all are. And if you think you cannot donate organs because of medical or other reasons, please consider discussing this with the United Network of Organ Sharing (UNOS) or your regional area organ bank. They may be able to provide you with valuable information to make an informed choice driven by facts not fear or uncertainty. There is so much more to accomplish.

Go to: http://www.unos.org/ and see the website for UNOS to learn more about what they do and the many ways you can become involved. Even if there is definitive reason why you cannot donate organs, there are other ways you can help by supporting the work of UNOS or your local organ donation organization. Please, donate life.

How to Help

Anyone who is interested in finding out how to become a donor or to research information about Donate Life America is invited to their website. A screen shot of their page follows: